M

D0287765

158.1 Acker.L
Ackerman, Laurence D., 1950-
The identity code

DATE DUE

APR 1 0 2006	
APR 2 8 2006	
AUG 14 2006	
MAY 2 6 2007	

ᴱMCO, INC. 38-2931

FEB 1 4 2006

ALSO BY LARRY ACKERMAN

*Identity Is Destiny: Leadership and the
Roots of Value Creation*

THE
IDENTITY
CODE

THE IDENTITY CODE

THE 8 ESSENTIAL QUESTIONS FOR FINDING

YOUR PURPOSE AND PLACE

IN THE WORLD

LARRY ACKERMAN

RANDOM HOUSE

NEW YORK

EVANSTON PUBLIC LIBRARY
1703 ORRINGTON AVENUE
EVANSTON, ILLINOIS 60202

The Identity Code is a work of nonfiction.
Some names and identifying details have been changed.

Copyright © 2005 by Laurence Ackerman

All rights reserved.

Published in the United States by Random House, an imprint of
The Random House Publishing Group, a division of
Random House, Inc., New York.

RANDOM HOUSE and colophon are registered
trademarks of Random House, Inc.

The Identity Circle as depicted on the book jacket was designed by Bruno Nesci.

Library of Congress Cataloging-in-Publication Data
Ackerman, Larry.
The identity code : The 8 essential questions for finding your
purpose and place in the world / Larry Ackerman.
p. cm.
Includes bibliographical references.
ISBN 1-4000-6417-1 (alk. paper)
1. Self-perception.   2. Vocation.   I. Title

BF697.5.S43 A25 2005
158.1—dc22   2005048955

Printed in the United States of America
on acid-free paper

www.atrandom.com

2 4 6 8 9 7 5 3 1

First Edition

Book design by Jo Anne Metsch

FOR MAX

Courage, always.

CONTENTS

Contents

THE
IDENTITY
CODE

THE IDENTITY CIRCLE

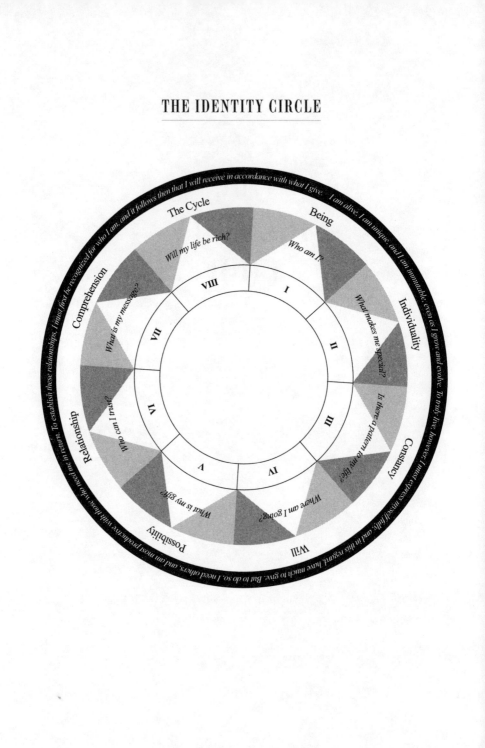

The Cycle

Being

Comprehension

Individuality

Relationship

Constancy

Possibility

Will

Will my life be rich?

Who am I?

What is my message?

What makes me special?

Who can I trust?

Is there a pattern to my life?

What is my gift?

Where am I going?

I am alive. I am unique and I am immutable, even as I grow and evolve. To truly live, however, I must express myself fully, and in this regard, have much to give. But to do so, I need others, and am most productive with those who need me in return. To establish these relationships, I must first be recognized for who I am, and it follows then that I will receive in accordance with what I give.

I II III IV V VI VII VIII

YOUR IDENTITY JOURNEY:

Making This Book Work for You

This book is designed to introduce you to yourself. Not the person you see in the mirror, physically speaking, or the one people necessarily interact with every day, but the person inside. The powerful one. The one who knows more than you realize about your unique capacities and whose ability to create value in this world—and get rewarded for it in return—is remarkable.

Each part of this book will guide you a bit further on your identity journey: first inside yourself, and then outside, into the world at large. You will find your identity, explore it, and then apply it to how you live.

The first part of this book will help you understand what identity is all about and the magnificent force it is in how it shapes human life.

Take heart from this discussion, knowing that you're not alone in taking the identity journey, nor in facing the challenges it poses.

Each of the next eight parts presents you with a question. As you answer these questions, your identity will gradually become clear. It will become the foundation upon which to make truly meaningful decisions about what work is right for you, how to build and maintain relationships that matter, and even what interests and hobbies make sense for you.

It is important for you to know how each of the eight questions unfolds, so you can follow your progress as you move along your identity journey. Understanding the simple structure of these eight parts will enable you to ready yourself for what comes next.

The story

Each question begins with a brief story about someone whose life has been deeply affected by his or her identity. Sometimes the outcome is positive and uplifting and will fill you with hope. In other situations, the result is sad and may leave you feeling unsettled, if not unhappy.*

Take from these stories insights and lessons that make sense to you.

The promise

Every story is followed by a discussion about the particular promise contained in answering the question at hand and the challenges we all face in "getting to" that promise. This discussion reveals many of the feelings you are likely to encounter as you wrestle with the question.

Use this discussion as a way to understand yourself better and accept yourself more fully.

The pathways

The next section will help you understand what you must do to realize the promise each answer holds. These are the main pathways into your identity, and will help you figure out how to apply your identity to your life. Within each of these pathways I offer guidelines, which help make these pathways more concrete.

Use this section as a way to ready yourself for change.

*The names of the people I refer to in this book are fictitious, with selected exceptions.

The exercises: the Identity Mapping™ *process* ⋆

Each of the eight questions concludes with a series of personal identity exercises, which will help you decipher your identity code. These exercises are designed to respond to, and expand upon, the pathways and guidelines presented in that part of the book. Taken together, these exercises constitute the *Identity Mapping process.* Consider this process a way to jump-start the work you will need to do on your own to make your identity the guiding force in your life.

The Identity Mapping process contains many exercises. Some are very simple to understand, while others are more challenging. Some of them will be fairly easy to do, while others will take a great deal of time. There is no need to feel as though you must complete them all in order to live by your identity code. In each part of the book, find the exercises that are most appealing to you, that speak to you on a personal level. Complete those first. You can always go back to other exercises when you are ready to do so.

Completing these exercises will require that you create a personal identity journal, which you will use as you move through the book. Your journal can take many forms. It can be a hand-tooled, leather-bound diary; a pad of paper; or your computer—whatever feels right to you. Consider your journal a "living document," meaning that you can return to any portion of it anytime you wish, adding to or changing its content.

These Identity Mapping exercises will take time. Don't rush the process. The more time you take to consider, and reconsider, your answers, the better and more meaningful they will be.

Feel free to ask for help. Find a partner. Although doing the work is up to you, it is easy to be distracted or get discouraged at times. Consider finding a friend, someone you trust, who is willing

⋆Identity Mapping™ is a trademark of Laurence D. Ackerman.

to help you get to the root of some of the answers you seek, someone who will be there to provide the encouragement you need, if
and when you need it.

*Use the Identity Mapping process as a starting point from which to move
forward on your own.*

THE MYTH OF PERSONAL FREEDOM
AND THE MEANING OF IDENTITY

LIFE HAS ORDER

The idea that you can be whatever you want to be in life is a myth that tortures people needlessly. It forces you to follow false trails such as money, fame, or family approval, or to stay the course out of sheer desperation. It eats at the very core of your being. Why? Because it lacks integrity; it simply isn't true.

Why we succeed or fail on the path we choose in life, and why we feel basically good or bad about the choices we make along the way, isn't a random event. You can't assign credit or blame to how you were raised. Or chalk it up to the luck of the draw. Or to being in the right place at the right time. Or to any other explanation that avoids the truth.

From the time we are born, we are told by loving parents, devoted teachers, well-meaning friends, and larger-than-life public figures and celebrities that we can be anything we want to be. We can be that international airline pilot, that wealthy business entrepreneur, that Nobel Prize–winning scientist, maybe even that first female president or other head of state, if we aim high, work hard, and stay the course.

The promise of personal freedom is very seductive. Boosting our egos, it fires our imaginations and fills us with hope, confidence, and drive. We come to believe we are free to make choices

7

about our lives that are wide open, unrestricted by anything except, perhaps, our responsibility at some point to care for others—our families or aging parents, for instance.

From an early age, we swallow this elixir eagerly. Without thinking, we let it coat our way of life. Years later, as we start to consider vocations and careers, we follow this now deep-seated dream in earnest, the dream that the only order life has is the order we give it.

Lying in bed late at night, or as you sit on an airplane as a young executive, or contemplate alternatives for your college major, graduate work, or post–high school life, you look out into the world and ask the question *What do I want to do? I am free. Where do I want to go?* The possibilities seem endless. You are drunk with possibilities. They can be overwhelming.

For all the promise they hold, these questions can gnaw at you. Especially when the answers aren't obvious. Or when the answer that seems obvious at first doesn't necessarily make you feel good. It is then, in these sobering moments, that freedom loses some of its seductive charm. It is under these circumstances that you wake up to your desire for some frame of reference you can call upon to help you decide what to do—what is *right* to do, for you.

In the midst of this budding turmoil, some people continue to hold fast to their dream. They decide, for instance, that being wealthy is the most important thing, so they doggedly pursue jobs in investment banking or as business financiers. Others feel the obligation to walk in their father's or mother's footsteps, and so steadfastly follow the path their lineage suggests. Still others have invested years in a particular field—politics, the arts, science, journalism, sales, accounting, carpentry—and can't imagine walking away from it after so long. *All those years,* you think; *it's too late to change.*

Despite how outwardly successful they may be, the question remains: Are these people happy? It is the only question that matters. By "happy" I do not mean you are always cheerful, or pleasant, or even nice. I mean that you are at peace with yourself. You understand your unique capacities and live according to them. You are *happy* being who you are among others in the world.

If they are truly fortunate, some people really will be happy, down to the very roots of their souls. Others, however, whether they wind up rich or poor, will insist they are happy but know better. For them, something is missing; something grates at them, inside. But they are afraid to admit it, to themselves as well as to others.

> *By "happy" I mean you are at peace with yourself. You are* happy *being who you are among others in the world.*

Unbridled freedom weighs you down. Stress takes hold: *I need to make a decision about my life, but can't.* Guilt surfaces: *I wonder what's wrong with me, why I can't figure out what to do.* Depression filters into your bones: *I am lost. I am in pain.* Despair grips your heart: *I don't know where I'm going; I must be a failure.*

The myth of personal freedom—the idea that you are at liberty to pick whatever path in life you want—is the unspoken agony of the modern person. It ignores the fact that life has order, and that that order bears heavily upon your choices—on what makes sense to do with the time you have. The good news is that although you can't be anything you want to be, you have more potential than you know.

The order I am speaking about is contained in a code, the *identity code*. Much like our biological, genetic code, our identity code is born into each of us, providing a complete map of how we, as human beings, are designed to function—of how we are supposed to live—when we are living according to who we are. Within the framework your identity provides, life's seeming boundaries melt away. Genuine freedom is yours.

By "identity" I mean the unique characteristics that, in combination with one another, define your potential for creating value in this world; that is, for making a contribution that springs naturally from the core of your being and touches the lives of others in positive ways.

Living according to your identity doesn't happen automatically. How our lives unfold isn't predetermined. Identity isn't a form of fatalism, where no matter what you do your life is destined to turn out a certain way. It is the opposite. It is up to each of us to learn who we are, and then to act upon this knowledge in ways that enable us to realize our potential. We are responsible for what happens to us in life. We are responsible for making identity our framework for living.

> *You can't be anything you want to be, but you have more potential than you know.*

Our identity code isn't obvious. We can't see it. Our physical senses are inadequate when it comes to comprehending it. But it is there, waiting to be discovered and embraced.

Crack your identity code and the contours of your life will shift. You will not only come out stronger, you will come out *larger.* Larger in heart, larger in influence, larger in your capacity to love and be loved.

You will find the right friends. You will marry smarter. You will discover the right line of work or field of study, and the place to practice it. You will parent better. You will honor the right heroes and worship the right gods. You may even live longer. You will understand the *why* of your own life.

THE EIGHT QUESTIONS

The identity code is found in the answers to eight questions. These questions are:

Who am I?
What makes me special?
Is there a pattern to my life?
Where am I going?
What is my gift?
Who can I trust?
What is my message?
Will my life be rich?

At first glance, these questions may appear similar to any number of other life-shaping questions people ask themselves in the course of their lives. Questions like *Why am I here?* Or, *What is my purpose?* But these eight questions aren't arbitrary. They come from one source: a series of eight natural laws—*the Laws of Identity*—which are part of the very constitution of nature and govern our lives like clockwork.

Natural laws aren't a new phenomenon. They've been with us for aeons. Our instinct for self-preservation and innate love of our offspring, for instance, are also natural laws that shape our universe, just as the Laws of Identity do. Natural laws are all about action and reaction. For instance, when you feel threatened, you automatically defend yourself. If your child is in trouble, you instinctively determine how best to help him or her. Your response is involuntary. It is entirely *natural*.

The idea that there are laws of nature that frame the choices we make in life, and their inevitable impact on our well-being, may seem far-fetched to you. Most people believe the opposite to be true: that life is a freewheeling experience, and you can never know what's coming next.

> *You will unearth capacities you never knew you had.*

Yet we readily accept that there are laws that hold sway over the physical world, such as the laws of thermodynamics, which can be scientifically validated. When it comes to identity, and the profound impact it has on one's life, there is no doubt in my mind that equally powerful laws exist in nature, even though they can't be demonstrated empirically.

The effects of the Laws of Identity can be seen, for instance, by observing the apparent quality of your own life: How content or discontented are you? How grounded are you as an individual? Would you say that you are your "own person," or do you frequently follow the crowd? Do you stand up publicly for what you believe in, or acquiesce to others' opinions? The answers to these questions provide clues to whether or not you are living in harmony with who you are. The closer you are to living according to your identity, the closer you are to being in sync with the natural laws I am referring to. The opposite is equally the case.

Not only do the eight questions I put forward flow directly from the Laws of Identity, but how I present them—their sequence—is crucial to cracking your identity code. The sequence of these questions builds in a way that tells a story about how life develops when it is lived through the lens of identity.

Without giving away the ending, I will tell you this: The journey you will take begins by finding and embracing a feeling for life you have most likely never experienced before. The feeling I am referring to can't be reached through any of the five physical senses we take for granted: touch, sight, hearing, smell, or taste.

Once you have located this feeling, you will wind your way through a period of self-discovery, during which you will unearth capacities you never knew you had—and come face-to-face with trials you never knew existed.

Finally, as your identity becomes clear, taking on form and meaning, you will arrive at a place where you are filled with passion, conviction, and serenity—a place you will recognize, finally, as *home*.

In the course of this book, I will illustrate how each of the Laws of Identity, and the question it holds, shapes a crucial piece of your identity code, and how together these laws add up to a fundamental reality that embraces us all.

DISCOVERING THE LAWS OF IDENTITY

In the summer of 1996, I was vacationing with my family at a ranch in Colorado. Sitting alone in the anteroom of our cabin, my mind drifted back to a conversation I had had with a friend some months earlier. This was the gist of our conversation: I was explaining my belief that there is more to the idea that every person is unique than that truism conveys. My assertion wasn't casual. I meant it literally. *There is more at work in the forces of human nature than we know.* It has to be that way, I reasoned, because people are born with identities that shape who they are and, by extension, affect what they do with their lives. That conversation rolled around in my mind for well over an hour, as I watched the sun arc across the aspens behind our cabin.

Suddenly, I understood what I had been struggling to say: that there are laws of nature that exist simply as a result of being human

and that knowing these laws is the key to understanding our uniqueness and potential as individuals. That revelation changed my life
forever.

In the hours and days that followed, that insight absorbed nearly
all of my energy. I had opened the floodgates to a well of knowledge within me that had lain dormant for decades. One perception
cascaded into another in rapid succession.

In my state of hyperawareness, I sensed the concreteness of
my own identity. I could almost feel it pulsating inside me. It was
the *soft rock* at the center of what made me, me. Not only did my
identity seem tangible, it also appeared to contain a particular
structure—a structure, I realized, that was somehow linked to the
natural laws I now knew existed. The image that came to my mind
in that moment was beautiful. I felt I was watching the bud of a
rose open suddenly, unfolding its petals all at once to reveal a small,
glowing sphere at its center.

> *There are laws of nature that exist simply
> as a result of being human.*

By definition, a person's identity isn't something to be unfurled
like a flower, in ways that expose its hidden parts. The opposite
is true: identity is the most perfectly integrated expression of a
human being there is. Our identity presents nothing less than the
"whole" picture of who we are capable of becoming as individuals. The fact that I was now able to glimpse its remarkable composition only heightened my sense of anticipation.

In that instant, I understood that the structure my identity contained illuminated not just its beauty but its extraordinary power as
well. If I could decipher my identity, I imagined, I would discover
the secrets it held—secrets about my special strengths and true pas-

sions, and what they suggested in terms of which path to follow and which ones to avoid.

Two days later, sitting by a river near our cabin, I watched intently as the trees, the mountains, the cobalt-blue sky, and the late-day sun combined to produce their predictable splendor. From where I sat, it was easy to confirm that life is exquisitely beautiful, as far as the eye can see. But it had taken a different kind of sight for me to recognize how beautifully ordered life is at the core of our beings, where the essence of our selves is formed.

> *Your identity presents the "whole" picture of who you are capable of becoming as an individual.*

Identity is beautiful and it is powerful. The natural laws I discerned in the summer of 1996 have proven to be as universally absolute, inescapable, and predictive in their effect on life as the laws of physics, which govern the external world. These are the Laws of Identity:

    I. The Law of Being
       An individual's ability to live depends first upon defining one's self as separate from all others.

    II. The Law of Individuality
       A person's natural capacities invariably fuse into a discernible identity that makes that person unique.

    III. The Law of Constancy
       Identity is fixed, transcending time and place, while its manifestations are constantly changing.

    IV. The Law of Will
       Every individual is compelled to create value in accordance with his or her identity.

V. *The Law of Possibility*
Identity foreshadows potential.

VI. *The Law of Relationship*
Individuals are inherently relational and relationships are only as strong as the natural alignment between the identities of the participants.

VII. *The Law of Comprehension*
An individual's various capacities are only as valuable as the perceived value of the whole of that individual.

VIII. *The Law of the Cycle*
Identity governs value, which produces wealth, which fuels identity.

These laws are the same for everyone. They shape our lives and fortunes even when we aren't conscious of their presence. They are the foundation of the eight questions I presented earlier, the answers to which reveal your identity code.

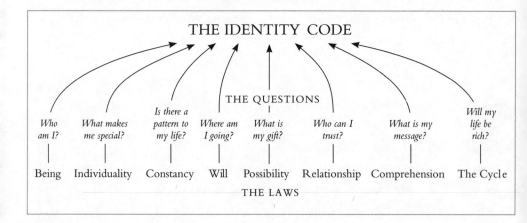

Living by your identity code holds out the promise of a life steeped in authenticity. It will provide you with a place to stand that is unwavering and rock solid, no matter how many turns your life may take. Consider this place your center of gravity. From here, you can move out, knowing that you will always be able to find and return to it. You can try new things, because when you do you will automatically assess them through the lens of your identity. Instinctively, you will know whether they make sense for you.

Your identity code allows you, like a skilled musician, the freedom to improvise—to change the key, tempo, or harmonies of your life—because you know how the notes ultimately fit together. You are always able to return to the melody line that is your life's original theme.

Living through your identity opens up possibilities you might never otherwise have seen—possibilities that are more expansive, and yet safer, than attempting to swim in uncharted waters. For all of these possibilities are anchored by the unique characteristics that make you who you are.

Getting to the answers that inform your identity code is a challenging task. There are no obvious guideposts for coming up with them. Once found, however, the answers are exhilarating; they hold out the prospect of true happiness.

The very first step is to recognize that your identity is an inherently positive force. Over the years, I have come to regard identity as the most powerful human force on earth. It is made powerful because it contains the seeds of all things valuable and worthwhile in you. And because identity reveals your potential to contribute, it is your connection with the world.

I have been asked many times whether I've ever known anyone whose identity was "bad," and, if so, what, if anything, could be done about it. *No.* I know of no such people, nor do I believe it is even possible for such a person to exist. What I believe happens all the time, however, is this: we are raised in families, communities, and societies that compel us to behave in ways that aren't always in sync with who we are. In order to comply with the demands our environment imposes, we develop beliefs about who we must become in order to survive. In turn, these beliefs influence how we live.

> *Recognize that your identity is an inherently positive force.*

So, figuratively speaking, we twist ourselves into knots. We deny our most deeply held values. We say yes when we mean no. We leave our true selves orphaned in the corners of our being. We do these things in order to get along with others, in order to be accepted by the people we need, or feel we need.

It is the false beliefs we unconsciously manufacture, and the actions they spawn, that get in the way of who we are at our core. Through no fault of our own, we lose touch with our identities.

Some people stray so far from themselves that they deny such a thing as "identity" even exists. But it does. In fact, identity is everywhere, making its mark in big ways and small ways, outside us as well as within us, whether we realize it or not.

IDENTITY IS ALL AROUND US

Since the beginning of recorded time, for as long as human beings have existed, our sense of identity has played a central role in how we live, in the decisions we make, and in the outcomes those decisions have on the fates of individuals, including ourselves, on families, on organizations, even on nations.

Wars have been fought over matters of identity. Consider, for instance, the war that raged for years between Catholics and Protestants in Northern Ireland, or the persistent Israeli-Palestinian conflict in the Middle East. In both cases, and in many more, each side believes passionately in a way of life that reflects its particular view of how the world works. This worldview includes how people define what is right and wrong; indeed, what is worth defending to the death. In other words, who they are and who they are not.

Identity is a subject that finds its way into all walks of life. In the world of art, young children draw primitive pictures depicting how they see themselves. Hands, lips, eyes, hair, and a hundred other features offer subtle clues to who they believe they are. Among the great artists, Picasso, for example, painted cubist portraits of people in ways that dramatized their personalities in unique, and often shocking, ways.

In our relationships, identity plays a particularly influential role. In families, we instinctively look for signs of how someone is or is not like someone else: a son to his father, a daughter to her mother, a brother to his sister.

In the workplace, we often find ourselves assessing how we fit in. We wonder about whether we share the same values as our employer or our boss. And, in turn, whether we actually belong where we are or, even more basically, whether we should be doing what we're doing to make a living.

> *Sometimes you wonder whether you actually belong where you are.*

Wherever people walk, identity follows, creating a landscape all its own. It is a landscape we all inhabit and it extends as far as the eye can see. For all the examples I could share with you, there are a few that illustrate particularly well just how pervasive identity is in our lives. Let me take you on a brief tour of the identity landscape, in three areas that affect us all: religion, the field of human psychology, and the media.

Many people find their identity in their religion, no matter what their faith may be. Here is a snapshot of how each of the world's three great monotheistic religions—Christianity, Judaism, and Islam—views identity.

In the Christian tradition, an individual's identity begins with the understanding that he or she is a child of God, and that God has intentionally created him or her out of His love and for the express purpose of having a relationship with God.

Because God loves us, Christianity says, He has endowed us with gifts that are to be used to honor Him. God has also given us free will to decide how, and even if, we will use those gifts. Our identity, then, as a beloved child of God calls for us to recognize our uniqueness as a child of God. It calls for us to use our gifts to the greater good of both ourselves and the world at large. Those who are unable, or unwilling, to recognize and utilize these gifts often struggle in life, ending up frustrated and unfulfilled.

Unfortunately, people who choose not to embrace their God-given identity frequently become estranged from Him and from other people as they grapple with their lack of identity. Often, these lost souls seek to fill their emptiness with activities that are misguided and, ultimately, unrewarding. However, individuals who embrace their identity as a child of God, and use their gifts to the greater good, experience a life filled with joy and fulfillment.

In short, from a Christian perspective, you discover your identity through your relationship with the triune God (God the father; God the Son, Jesus Christ; and God the Holy Spirit). There are many verses from the Old Testament that suggest how one's identity flows from God. The passage in Exodus 4:10–12 illuminates this view eloquently.

But Moses said to the Lord, "O my Lord, I have never been eloquent, neither in the past nor even now that you have spoken to your servant; but I am slow of speech and slow of tongue." Then the Lord said to him, "Who gives speech to mortals? Who makes them mute or deaf, seeing or blind? Is it not I, the Lord? Now go and I will be with you and teach you what you are to speak."

The Jewish view of identity offers its own way of understanding who you are. Jews celebrate the individual in his or her own right. The idea is that each of us is responsible for what happens to us in life. We were created in God's image and are free to be ourselves, to use the talents, skills, and passions that make each of us unique. It is entirely up to us, not God, however, to find our way, to create purpose in our lives for our benefit and the benefit of others.

Here is a passage from Mishnah Sanhedrin 4:5 taken from *A Rabbinic Anthology.* It cites a different verse from the Old Testament that celebrates human individuality, as it also celebrates the "greatness of God."

But a single man was created to proclaim the greatness of God, for man stamps many coins with one die, and they are all like to one another; but God has stamped every man with the die of the first man, yet not one of them is like his fellow. Therefore, everyone must say, for my sake was the world created.

For all the power and responsibility we have to shape our own lives, the Jewish religion tempers that power with a sense of humility. There is a midrash—a story—that says that when God set out to create the first humans, He chose dirt from the earth's "four corners": black, red, yellow, and white. The first humans were created from the earth's soil and contained within them the four colors, so that no one could later say that "because I am white, red, black, or yellow, I am better than anyone else."

In Islam, the notion of identity is defined by surrendering one's self entirely to God. Muslims express their identity by being obedient to God—Allah—whose divine will orders the universe and tells us how we are to live, for some Muslims even indicating what they are to eat, how they are to dress, and how they are to sleep.

Expressing their identities in practical terms calls for Muslims to perform their religious duties, such as reciting the five daily ritual prayers and giving alms to those in need. In short, Muslims derive their identities as creatures of God, from the creator of the world and humanity.

There is a well-known verse from the Koran, the "throne verse," that conveys the totality of Allah's influence:

God, there is no god but He, the Living, the Everlasting. Slumber seizes Him not, neither sleep; to Him belongs all that is in the heavens and the earth. Who is there that shall intercede with Him save by His leave? He knows what lies before them and what is after them, and they comprehend not anything of His knowledge save such as He wills. His Throne comprises the heavens and the earth; the preserving of them oppresses Him not; He is the All-high, the All-glorious.

Islam is more than just a religion; it is also a divinely ordered way of life, a community all its own. From this standpoint, your identity—your purpose here on this earth—is to testify to God's existence by submitting to His will, not just in religious terms but in everything you do.

Despite the differences among these three religions, all of them lead us to take our "identity cue" from God, who, in essence, sets the ground rules for helping us figure out who we are.

My aim in offering these three examples—there are many more—isn't to conclude which one of them is necessarily right. That decision is entirely up to you. My objective is simply to highlight how identity weaves its way into the fabric of the faiths we hold dear.

From another angle, identity constitutes a field of study. The subject of identity has captured the imagination of psychologists, scholars, and writers for generations. There are three people whose work I particularly admire and would like to introduce you to here. One of these people is Erik Erikson, a German-born psychologist who has been called the father of psychosocial development and the architect of identity.

> *Despite their differences, all of these religions lead us to take our "identity cue" from God.*

Erikson is often credited with helping to illuminate the roots of human identity and its impact on how we mature as individuals. One of his main contributions was to bridge the gap between human development, which focuses on meeting personal challenges, and the cultural factors that affect us all, such as our families, religions, and social environments. He explores these two forces in his groundbreaking book *Identity and the Life Cycle.* In it, Erikson describes identity as the blending of these two forces: an individual's ties with the particular values of his or her family, history, and heritage, and the traits that simply make each of us special.

From his studies, Erikson was able to map how people grow by developing their identities, beginning in infancy and early childhood, all the way through to adulthood and mature age. From Erikson's perspective, for all the change we may experience in our lives, our identity is a governing force that is with us always.

Another one of my favorite writers on the topic of human identity is the psychologist and scholar James Hillman. Hillman looks at identity through the lens of the soul. In fact, he wrote a book entitled *The Soul's Code,* subtitled *In Search of Character and Calling.* In his book, Hillman presents a vision of our selves that isn't defined by family relationships or other influences outside of us. He argues that what he terms "character" is fate and goes on to show how the soul, if given the opportunity, can assert itself at an early age.

In his book, Hillman presents the view that the fundamental essence of our individuality is within us from birth, shaping what we do as much as it is shaped by what we do. The "essence" he refers to can have many names. Some call it "genius." Others have named it "spirit," "daimon," and even "guardian angel." Call it what you will, it is identity by another name: that singularly unique set of characteristics, formed over time, that makes you who you are.

Our identity is a governing force that is with us always.

Finally, I'd like to mention M. Scott Peck. Peck, a medical doctor and psychiatrist, is probably best known as the author of *The Road Less Traveled,* one of the most widely read works on human behavior and spirituality. It is a beautiful book, filled with a love of humankind and a deep appreciation for the fact that life isn't easy. In fact, Peck's main premise is that life, literally, is hard and that accepting this truth is the first step in being able to deal with it.

One of Peck's most haunting ideas, as far as personal identity is concerned, ties together the notion of consciousness with God. In his book, there is a section entitled "The Evolution of Consciousness." I have drawn together selected passages from this section that provide an intriguing perspective on the true meaning of personal identity.

Peck's ideas aren't necessarily easy to digest; they require a bit of concentration in order to be understood. But they are powerful and fascinating. Follow his logic, as I present it here:

The word "conscious" is derived from the Latin prefix *con*, meaning "with" and the word *scire*, meaning "to know." To be conscious means "to know with." But how are we to understand this "with"? To know with *what*? We have spoken of the fact that the unconscious part of our mind is the possessor of extraordinary knowledge. It knows more than we know, "we" being defined as our conscious self. And when we become aware of a new truth, it is because we recognize it to be true; we re-know that which we knew all along.

But we still have not explained how it is that the unconscious possesses all this knowledge, which we have not yet consciously learned . . . I know of no hypothesis as satisfactory as the postulation of a God who is intimately associated with us—so intimately that He is part of us. If you want to know the closest place to look for grace, it is within yourself. If you desire wisdom greater than your own, you can find it inside you . . . To put it plainly, our unconscious is God.

The point is to become God while preserving consciousness. If [we do], then God will have assumed a new life form. This is the meaning of our individual existence. We are born that we might become, as a conscious individual, a new life form of God.

Peck's main message is that to know who you are at the core of your being is to know God. After reading *The Identity Code* it will be up to you to decide whether this view of identity aligns with your own.

Although he wasn't officially a psychologist by trade, there is one other person I'd like to bring up now who was a natural when it came to understanding human identity, and whose words have influenced millions of people over time. His name is Socrates and the words are "Know thyself."

Although other Greek philosophers are credited with having said these words, Socrates is considered first among them. In fact, Apollo's oracle of Delphi identified Socrates as being the wisest of all men. He understood that the first thing someone had to do, before they could know *what* to do, was to understand who they were; they needed to know their identity.

Socrates recognized the depth of the challenge contained in those two little words. He knew that if you didn't understand your identity, you would wind up lost. On the positive side, he recognized that if you stayed true to who you are, you would have the foundation you need to make the right decisions. Socrates was, indeed, a wise man.

Identity is a topic that is constantly in the news. I have spent many years collecting articles on identity. My habit began sometime ago, quite innocently, when I realized that so many news stories revolved around this subject. At first, I was amused at the random references to identity in the titles of articles. Over time, I came to see that the theme of identity wasn't just an occasional reference; it recurred, day after day, week after week, month after month, in a wide variety of mainstream newspapers and magazines.

> ## *"Know thyself."*

The nature of these articles was wide-ranging. Some of them were utterly simple, even silly. One, for example, discussed the identity of a thin-skinned cucumber, described as "green and a little confused." The story was about Persian cucumbers, which were actually being grown in Israel, Mexico, and California, ultimately to be sold in New York City.

Other articles were poignant. I vividly recall the story of a priest who felt like he had lost his sense of self following the destruction of his village in Poland in World War II. For a quarter of a century, he had been one with the people of that small town and, by some stroke of fortune, had survived the onslaught of the Nazis, when most others had not.

His story was movingly told. There was no happy ending, however. The article described the priest's struggle—he was now in his late eighties—to "redefine his identity" in ways that went beyond the town he had served for so long. What finally transpired was left to the reader's imagination, as the writer was unable to offer a conclusion. The article ended with a sense of grief that was, at best, leavened by a modicum of hope.

In my office, I have turned two large walls into a monument to identity. Together, I call them my *identity wall*. They are covered with articles and advertisements in which identity is the central theme. I add to my collection regularly. It is easy to do so, given the sheer number of stories that revolve around identity.

Many of these articles have been posted on my wall now for years and show the markings of age; they are dog-eared and yellowed from being exposed to sunlight and the air. In my eyes, their parchmentlike quality only adds to their authenticity, which is what identity is all about.

> *Authenticity is what identity is all about.*

Here is a smattering of titles from my identity wall. They are taken from a cross section of newspapers and magazines and cover a wide spectrum of subjects.

Identity in nations and places

"Many in Guyana Worry About Loss of Identity to Brazil"

"A City Seeks Its Identity Atop a Spire of Debate" (an article about Tacoma, Washington)

Identity in sports

"Mixing Street Tastes off the Court with a Button-down Approach on It. Elton Brand Is Infusing Los Angeles's Other Team with a New Identity" (a story about Elton Brand's impact on the Los Angeles Clippers basketball team)

"On Giants, New Faces and a New Identity" (an article describing how a host of new players is giving the New York Giants football team a makeover)

Identity in our personal lives

"Identity Shift" (an article about midlife career changes)

"Officials Worried over a Sharp Rise in Identity Theft" (an article about the rising problem of people stealing credit card and other personal information)

Identity in food and wine

"Chilean Sea Bass: More Than an Identity Problem" (an article about overfishing the Patagonian toothfish, a tasty, but ugly, fish)

"Syrah Seeks Its Own Identity" (an article about the wine varietal Syrah)

Identity in the arts and literature

"Museum Seeks an Identity" (an article about the Cooper-Hewitt Museum in New York City)

"Identity—The Scariest Movie Since The Ring*"* (an advertisement for the movie *Identity*)

"An Identity Crisis for Norman Rockwell's America" (from the book *Who Are We? The Challenge to America's National Identity* by Samuel Huntington)

Identity in higher education

"Pulitzer Winner Tells New Students to 'Rummage' for Their Own Identities" (an article about Tony Horwitz addressing Brandeis University's class of 2007)

Identity in business

"Toyota to Change Design Approach to Clarify Identity"

"Philip Morris Identity Crisis Never Seems to Go Away" (an article about another company that owned the name Altria, Philip Morris's new corporate name)

There is one more stop I would like to make on this tour of the identity landscape before moving on. It is a place where identity finds an unlikely home—that is, in the world of fables and fairy tales, where, as children, we first begin to consider who we are. Here is a fairy tale that illustrates my point.

A family of ducks was tending a bunch of freshly hatched eggs, as they do every spring. One particular egg was large and ugly. A couple of these ducks thought it was a turkey egg at first. It was definitely a strange-looking object that some ducks immediately wanted to kick out of the brood.

The egg in question was pecked at by a few of the ducks. It was beaten by chickens who happened to stroll by and see it. And it was kicked by the little girl who fed the poultry on the farm where all of these feathered creatures lived.

Finally, the egg hatched and a strange birdlike creature emerged. It looked nothing like the ducks among which it had lain for so long. The ducks then asked this creature, "What kind of duck are you?" The odd-looking creature shook his small, furry head. He couldn't answer their question and didn't know what to say. Feeling thoroughly rejected, he went out into the world on his own, into the thick of winter.

The next spring, he found himself in a garden. As he was wandering around, he came across some beautiful swans. He was compelled to swim to them; for some reason, he found them irresistible. Still, he was scared, thinking all along that they might kill him because he was so ugly compared to them.

Rather than shoo him away or attack him, they rushed to meet him. At first, he was startled. Then, looking at his reflection in the water, he saw that he was one of them. He didn't know what to do. He was elated. Rustling his feathers, he curved his long neck and cried out, "I never dreamed of such happiness when I was an ugly duckling."

> *Identity is everywhere.*

The story of *The Ugly Duckling,* by Hans Christian Andersen, is a classic tale of identity, of discovering who you are and, in turn, where you truly belong. In my work with people and organizations, I have come to believe that there are millions of "ugly ducklings" in the world, who aren't ugly at all. They simply haven't yet found the swan within themselves.

MY IDENTITY, MY LIFE

You may be wondering how I came to know what I do about identity. Where, you might ask, does my knowledge come from? What are my credentials?

I make my living as an identity consultant. I help organizations, and the men and women who lead these organizations, come to terms with who they are, what they stand for, and what to do about it. I bring them face-to-face with their uniqueness, and the potential it implies.

My clients are among the most influential companies on earth. They include Fidelity Investments, Lockheed Martin, Boise Cascade, Dow, the European beverage giant Interbrew, Norsk Hydro, a century-old Norwegian industrial concern, and the American consumer icon Maytag. Together, they influence the lives of millions of people who make their living in service to these organizations, and who often believe that their identities are, at least in part, tied to them.

If there is one thing I have found that the great majority of employees want, it is a sense of purpose that gives their work meaning beyond their paycheck. In part, it is my job to help make this happen, to everyone's benefit.

Over the past twenty-five years, I have spent countless hours talking to the people—employees, customers, investors, suppliers, community leaders—who are responsible for helping my clients find "happiness." Their happiness is measured by many things. Most certainly, money plays a big role. But I have found that an organization's sense of fulfillment, just like a person's, depends on other forms of wealth as well.

In an interview with a chief executive not long ago, I asked him what had led him to want to search for the identity of his institution. At first, he explained that investors were putting pressure on him to break up the company. It was composed of different businesses, which, on the surface, had little in common. As a result, shareholders felt that the various operations might perform better if they were run independently. He hoped, he said, that there was something to his one-hundred-year-old organization that might explain the value of the whole and, thus, the logic of keeping the company together.

> *Most people want in their work a sense of purpose,*
> *beyond their paycheck.*

After a moment's pause, the CEO looked away from me and down at the table where we were sitting. Slowly, he folded his hands together in front of him and continued to speak in carefully measured tones. The essence of what he said was this: for years, he had been struggling to answer employees' questions about what the company really stood for, what it was all about, beyond the lines of business it contained and the customers it served. His inability to provide what he felt was an adequate answer weighed on his conscience. How could he legitimately lead people if he couldn't answer such a basic question? As he spoke, my eyes met his and he said, "I need a North Star. I need to be able to point to what our purpose is beyond making a profit. If we have one, I need to know what our identity is."

I have had thousands of such conversations with people over the years. These discussions, and the insights they produced, have been the basis for meeting the unique challenges of each of my clients, whose value-creating potential is found in their identities. What I have learned is this: the needs of organizations are no different from the needs of people. The eight Laws of Identity that apply to human beings also apply to organizations. That is how I approach my work. It is the secret of my success.

I have other credentials as well, which in many ways have proven to be more powerful than my professional experience. Even more powerful, I believe, than the credentials one acquires through schooling or clinical training as a psychologist, or therapist. I am a man, a *human* to be exact, who has come to understand life firsthand through the lens of identity. Because of its profound influence on everything I am and do, I need to tell you my story.

To some people, my story will seem extreme. Some of you will think, *There, but for the grace of God, go I.* Others will quickly conclude that they have had no similar life experience and, therefore, my ideas about identity really don't apply to them. They would be mistaken. It isn't my experience that matters; what matters is what I learned about the power of human identity—in essence, what I learned about you.

My story revolves around all things visual: sight, vision, eyes, perception, seeing, discernment. Call it what you will, this is my world. When I was four years old I underwent eye surgery to correct a muscle problem; I was born cross-eyed. Medically speaking, the operation was a success, but during that operation the course of my life was altered forever.

I have no doubt that my parents tried, in advance of the surgery, to describe to me in loving, careful words what was to come. But it didn't matter. No four-year-old can understand the idea of surgery, no matter how compassionately it is presented to him or her.

The first moment I am able to recall is being on the operating table, looking around with a mix of childlike curiosity and growing trepidation. The doctors, nurses, and various assistants were moving about, preparing for the procedure in their businesslike, matter-of-fact way. The operating room was coming alive with activity. I, however, had no conception of what was going on, no earthly idea why I was there.

Lying on my back, a cold, tingly fear crept up along both sides of my body and settled firmly in my heart. I figured something must be wrong with me; after all, my parents had put me in this place of sick people. And if something was wrong with me, then I needed to be "fixed"; I needed an operation. As I saw it, my eyes were the problem. I say that because that is what my mother and father had told me; that was the reason they had brought me here: I was cross-eyed and that apparently wasn't okay. So, I concluded, it was my eyes that had gotten me into trouble. (Bad eyes!)

Suddenly, I saw my life in stark, black-and-white terms: *Fix my vision, fix myself.*

From that unconscious, unspoken moment on, my ability to see became paramount—my parents' love and acceptance hung in the balance and, as a helpless four-year-old, so did my very survival. Or so I believed.

Two completely different scenes unfolded at the same time. Each had its own set of characters, yet neither set of players was aware of the other. One scene was medical. It was composed of the doctors and nurses who simply went about doing their jobs. The other scene was psychological. I created it, second by second, as I took up my role at the center of this sudden maelstrom.

> *Suddenly, I saw my life in black-and-white terms:*
> Fix my vision, fix myself.

As I lay on the operating table, panic filled my heart. With a sense of indignation, I felt these words well up inside me: *No! Stop this! Leave me alone!* I strained to look over to the stainless-steel doors through which I had been wheeled into the room. From my prone position, I peered at the two portal-like windows in the doors, searching for my father. He never came. I felt abandoned. I was utterly helpless and alone.

To this day, I can recall being tethered to the operating table, canvas straps pulled snug across my chest and pelvis. I watched in terror as the gas mask was brought to my face. My control over myself had been torn away from me. I began repeating to myself, *Doesn't anyone care about me?* Quickly, however, a new question consumed me: *What is so wrong with me that I must be changed from who I am?* All I could figure was that my eyes were hopelessly flawed and, therefore, so was I. I sensed imminent death. *No!* I shouted to myself a second time. *Please, don't hurt me!* I begged, beneath the mask that muffled my growing horror.

At that excruciating instant, unable to breathe, part of me went away down a black hole—my "tunnel" to freedom and survival. I had abandoned my identity to save my life. At the instant I slipped away, however, in the midst of my living nightmare, I pledged to myself that I would return. *No!* I screamed for the third and last time. *I will not die! I will be back.*

> *What is so wrong with me that I must be changed from who I am?*

In the next moment, I tumbled headlong into another state of being, a state of consciousness I am now convinced exists in all of us, in some form or other. I crossed the divide between what we can see and sense in physical terms, and what is there to be "seen and sensed" on another plane.

I found myself in an absolutely silent, airless place. It was a meadow, to be exact, where I was completely alone. There was not another person in sight. Not another soul crossed my path. With calm, collected eyes, I took in everything around me: the meadow's waving grasses, trees in distant clusters, birds winging their way about the sky. There was no sound, no oxygen, in this place I now roamed. I was dead, but alive. The silence and my lack of breath were complete.

Despite my outer life—the one that connected me then, as now, to other people and the physical world—I wandered through my meadow timelessly and peacefully. It was safe. It was my new home.

Forty years passed before I became fully conscious of this experience. My will to "return" had remained alive. If I was to come back, I needed to know exactly what had happened to me. I needed to know what had led to my obsession to be whole again and, in recent years, to help others benefit from the trauma I had survived.

Since the day I slipped away, I have been at work, more unconsciously than not, to restore my integrity as a complete person. A supposedly routine medical procedure had forced me to confront the question *Who am I?* far sooner than I was prepared to do so. Reconnecting with my identity, and helping others do the same, has been the governing force in my life ever since.

The Laws of Identity I discerned in Colorado in the summer of 1996 were knowledge I had attained as a toddler, amid the flames of my "escape" from surgery. Sitting in the anteroom of my cabin that afternoon, four decades after my operation, I wrote down in earnest what I realized I had known all my life.

> *The silence and my lack of breath were complete.*

In purely technical terms, my eyes have always been a source of trouble for me—first at the age of four, and now in my fifties. Three operations to correct being cross-eyed and two corneal transplants, coupled with having monocular, rather than binocular, vision, attest to this fact. But then, as now, I chose to take a different route: if my eyes were technically unfixable, then I would find other ways to see.

Beginning as a toddler, searching for the meaning of what happened to me in that operating room, I have taken vision *inside* and made it—call it inner sight, or insight—a way of living. But not just insight in the general sense; rather, insight with a purpose.

In response to the ugly horror I endured as a child, I have come to look for beauty in all things. Certainly in the physical world, in nature, in light, in people—in all matter and form. But I also seek, and find, beauty in other things as well: in elegant ideas that alter patterns of thinking and behavior, in well-turned phrases that capture my imagination and take up permanent residence in my mind, even in the heroic deeds I read about every day, both large and small, that shape our fates.

My identity journey has been a long, sometimes trying, often joyous, always adventuresome trek. It has been worth the trip, for I know who I am; I know my purpose: *I am driven by the need to help people to see.* To see the futility of some actions and the power of others. To see one's potential as prescribed by his or her identity. To see the beauty in living according to who you are.

Do I know you well enough to tell you exactly how to decipher your own identity code? How to answer each of the eight questions? Certainly not. But I know this *about* you: You are stronger than you feel, wiser than you think, more powerful than you may care to admit, more courageous than you believe. Do not shrink from the opportunity to discover who you are. Honor yourself. Take the journey.

> *You are stronger than you feel, wiser than you think, more powerful than you may care to admit.*

THE FIRST QUESTION:

Who Am I?

THE LAW OF BEING

An individual's ability to live depends first upon
defining one's self as separate from all others.

*The thing that makes you exceptional is inevitably
that which must also make you lonely.*

—LORRAINE HANSBERRY

BRIAN

We all know them. We may even be one of "them": people
who, knowingly or not, live to please others.

These people's lives may be marked by the trappings of success:
big titles or jobs we may admire, membership in fancy clubs we have
never been invited to join, glamorous stage careers, lovely homes
and families worthy of a postcard. But their ready smiles betray less
happy truths. All of their apparent achievements add up to little. To
get what they have, these seemingly successful people have worked
hard to satisfy everyone but themselves. They've forgotten that

they too are "people worth pleasing." They have left themselves behind.

I am reminded of Brian, an old friend from college, whom I met in a Roadrunners Club in my junior year, and admired for his marathoning ability.

Brian was one of *them*. He made a career out of pleasing others. In all his jobs, he unfailingly represented other people's views. After graduate school, Brian held a number of increasingly important positions in a large, international public relations firm. Later, he became press secretary to one of the most colorful congressmen in Washington. Building on these successes, Brian was appointed executive director of a national trade association in the food industry. All of these posts shared one thing in common: they required serving others, a skill my friend had mastered.

If you look hard enough, you can usually find telltale cracks in the armor of success. Brian was no exception to this rule. Brian drank a lot. To my knowledge, he still does. I sense that Brian's need to make other people happy began long before I met him. Perhaps at home in Vermont, where he was raised.

> *You can usually find cracks in the armor of success.*

Now when I think about Brian running marathons, I don't imagine him running toward the finish line. Instead, I imagine him running *away*—from what, I do not know. I see him running far and fast, but never far or fast enough to separate himself from whatever haunts him.

My good friend never achieved the distance he needed to figure out who he was, apart from those he served. That is a distance, I am sure, that eludes him to this day.

GETTING TO THE PROMISE
OF AFFIRMATION

Who am I? is a question that has been asked in various ways by everyone from great philosophers such as Plato and Aristotle to decidedly not-so-famous people: that jumble of "regular folk" who make their lives in the far-flung cities, towns, and villages we call home. Asking the question *Who am I?* makes kin of us all.

At times, you may pose the question in calm, contemplative moments, like when you're strolling along the beach at sunset as waves lap at your feet. In these moments, arriving at the answer isn't necessarily the urgent matter; rather, it is a moment of reflection, a "time-out" from the incessant demands of your daily life. In this sense, asking the question *Who am I?* is like a small luxury you bestow upon yourself, much as you might allow yourself a favorite treat, but only on rare occasions.

At other times, you might ask the question amid the fires of growing despair. Your job has become meaningless and boring. Your daily routine seems tedious and empty. The affiliations you've relied upon to define yourself no longer seem sufficient.

Am I not a Jones, a Stern, a Tanaka, you may ask—the child of a good family? Am I not a loyal Christian, a pious Jew, a devout Muslim? Am I not American? Or Turkish? Or Japanese, or Indian? Am I not, at least, a hardworking employee? Are these things not enough? If not, *Who am I, then?* Not surprisingly, your question begs for an answer. It never comes.

In fact, you may be any combination of these things; for instance, a Jones, a Christian, and a hardworking American. But none of these labels answers the question *Who am I?* That is because, despite their importance in how you define yourself, these labels serve to mask, rather than reveal, who you are at your core. Apart from being a member of any of these groups, you are, in the words of Walt Whitman, "a simple, separate person," independent of the customs, cultures, and conventions society imposes.

This may be a difficult notion to grasp. It may confound your view of how the world works. It may even cause you to lose your balance, if not your way. Still, it is the truth. Embrace it and you will find fresh footing that is sturdier, and more reliable, than what you have experienced in the course of your life so far.

Don't be afraid that once you've stripped away the labels, there will be nothing there. Such fear is unfounded. You are not your labels. You simply *are*. Learn to appreciate yourself in your most elemental form, free, if only for a moment, of the social markings we all rely on to delineate where we fit in the world.

Locating this sense of self is like being born anew. At its fullest, this sensation will make everything around you seem intensely vibrant and animated—as though you are encountering life for the first time. What you are sensing, however, aren't the things around you; it is yourself in a heightened state of awareness. Discovering that you are here in the spiritual sense connects you to the very roots of consciousness: *I am here. I exist.*

As I was working to decipher my own identity code, I would often repeat to myself, *I am Larry Ackerman.* Not Larry, son of Jack and Anne. Not Larry, the American, the Jew, or the consultant, or any one of a dozen other labels I could claim. But, simply, Larry Ackerman, the man, the human being. This rudimentary exercise kept me centered. It kept me from taking the easy way out and just accepting the stamps society put on me, before I even knew that it had happened. Finding your "I" is the exhilarating and necessary first step in beginning your identity journey.

The answer to the question *Who am I?* brings with it the promise of affirmation—nothing less than the awakening of your spirit. It is no great feat to verify that you exist in physical terms. Your five senses do this for you automatically. It is something else entirely, however, to experience yourself as aware and awake, separate from the flesh, bones, and breath we take for granted as standard signs of life.

> *You are not your labels. You simply are.*

Experiencing this confirmation of life is a prelude to everything else you will learn and do in relation to your identity. Once you have found this feeling of life, you will be ready to discover your uniqueness as an individual and the potential it implies for how you ultimately engage the world.

DEFINE YOURSELF AS SEPARATE FROM ALL OTHERS

Within each of us lies the innate, if unconscious, knowledge that if we know who we are, we will know why we are here. We will have found our natural gyroscope, which will guide us to a wonderful place from which to engage life. On the strength of that gyroscope, all decisions will be wise decisions, and their outcomes, no matter what challenges or hardships may follow, will be the right ones.

It isn't surprising that the prospect of achieving such a keen state of being leads one to ask, *How can I discover who I am?*

The way to know who you are is by first *defining yourself as separate from all others.* Within the context of identity, separation isn't about being physically or emotionally remote from people—physical separation isn't especially difficult to achieve, if that is what you desire, and emotional connections are essential for strong relationships.

Separation is about putting some healthy distance between yourself and other people so you can step back and see, *really see,* yourself within the context of your relationships. How are you different from your best friend, your brother, or mother, in terms of your personality, your values, and your talents? Consider answering these questions to be an exercise in setting boundaries that mark out turf belonging just to you, no matter how close you are to others.

Think about separation as finding some space where you can slow down and look at yourself and others objectively. The aim is to see people—yourself included—through fresh eyes. The feeling separation evokes is similar to the feeling you might have when you learn, or see, something for the very first time. In that instant, you are exceptionally alert; all of your senses are operating on edge in an effort to comprehend what you have just encountered.

How can I discover who I am?

What you seek in separation is independence—the ability to think and act on your own and in your own best interests, despite what others may expect of you. Defining yourself as separate from others is about finding your own integrity as an individual. It gives you a place to live within relationships that is all your own, even in moments of greatest intensity: in the sweat of a crowded locker room after a come-from-behind victory; in heated conversation with your parent or child; or in making love, when there is, it seems, only one of you.

Put plainly, before you can know who you are, you need to know who you are not.

The act, even the prospect, of separation, however, can stir strong, unfamiliar emotions: misgivings and resistance, as well as exhilaration and hope. Each of these is a normal byproduct of the experience.

If you are like most people, the idea of separation will spark fear. Fear of being alone, of a kind of brutal rending from your daily routine and lifelines—the relationships you've come to count on as sources of social oxygen. But for all the apprehension you may at first experience, you will likely find that being able to "stand alone" strengthens you. Facing up to the initial discomfort that aloneness may bring is a sure sign of progress. Stay with it. It is part of your passage to discovery.

In your efforts to find separate space, you may feel guilty that you are turning your back on people who need you: family and friends, among others. This response is a natural result of caring about others. It is uncalled for, however. In fact, you are developing your powers as an individual in your own right. Whether it takes you six months or six years, operating from the special turf that is yours alone will enable you to contribute to those relationships as a stronger person, with more to give.

You may also feel you are being selfish by taking time to focus on separation, especially with the express intent of detaching yourself from others—parents, children, close friends, and associates—who have given you so much. Perhaps you are. But taking this time isn't self-indulgent; it is self-affirming. How can you give to others if you do not also give to yourself?

What you seek in separateness is independence.

The prospect of stripping yourself, even for a moment, of the various labels you have come to take for granted in your life, of exposing yourself to questions rather than answers, is, at the very least, anxiety-producing. It can make you feel as though there will be nothing there but yawning, uncharted space once the quilts and comforters of longstanding relationships are removed. But this isn't the case at all.

Know that the shivers you feel running down your spine as you consider entering your separate space are glimmers of life, not the coming of death. You are simply preparing the way, *your way,* for discovery. Your task is to clear the path so that the contours of your identity can become visible to your eye, unencumbered by the burden of others' expectations.

Look beyond your family's roots

From the time we are children, we find ourselves in the photographs that dot the shelves of our living rooms, our bedrooms, and the doors of our refrigerators. They surround us, reminding us of where we belong. Each snapshot lets us know we are part of a *family*—that special group of people that gives us a past, keeps us anchored in the present, and affords us shelter as we make our way in the world.

In your mirror, you see telltale signs of belonging. You recognize the small cleft in your father's chin, which now belongs to you as well. You gaze at yourself through the same blue eyes that make your mother's face shine. The waves in your grandfather's now silver hair have somehow found their way to you. You are, no doubt, part of this family.

Over Sunday dinners, you hear stories about great-aunts, great-uncles, and other long-dead ancestors whose hardheaded determination and spunk led them to succeed in the face of hardship. Sometimes those hardships were experienced two hundred years ago, on the plains of the untamed West. In other cases, they were lived on bread lines in the depths of the Great Depression. Either way, your family triumphed.

> *Taking time for yourself isn't self-indulgent; it is self-affirming.*

Listening intently, you take it all in, allowing the story to take root in your being. In the next instant, you naturally wonder, *Do I have any of those genes? Do I have that determination, that spunk, in me, too?* Yes, you conclude, you do. *I am them,* you think. And, in a flash, your family ties deepen.

Family stories aren't always triumphant. Sometimes they can be distressing, but their power to influence your view of who you are is no less intense. I recall stories my friend Brian told me about his upbringing in Vermont. His father, I recall, was pleasant, but unapproachable. Shaking hands was as affectionate as he would ever get with his son, a fact Brian mentioned to me numerous times.

Raised in a strict, somewhat formal family himself, his father told Brian stories about relatives who had struggled in vain to build various businesses. Inevitably, they'd wind up shuttering them after a couple of years and have to go back to work for someone else. As Brian described it, there was a kind of cloud over his family that seemed to follow them everywhere.

For Brian, the pictures of family that dotted the walls of his home were constant reminders of that cloud, despite the love he had for his parents and relatives. *Am I like them? Will that cloud find me? No doubt it will,* he may have concluded; *I am my family.*

For better or worse, our families color our sense of who we are, from the moment we are born. They wrap us in their successes, triumphs, victories, and blessings, as well as in their failures, struggles, and seeming curses. The lessons we take away from them tug at us, as though we have no choice but to follow the precedent they've set. But we do have a choice. In fact, for all the love and warmth our families may provide, we have an obligation to put some distance between ourselves and them, if only for a little while.

To get to know yourself as a separate person, you must attain a certain detachment from the people to whom you are closest—those individuals whose history and blood you share. Whether we are aware of it or not, our roots keep us tethered firmly, and sometimes blindly, to family, blocking our ability to see ourselves clearly.

I have spent countless hours in conversations with people, some well known to me and some barely known, who spoke proudly of generations of doctors, of filmmakers, of shoemakers, of automotive executives, of military men and women. But, in the end, they revealed little about themselves.

All along, I wondered, did they believe it? Did they define themselves solely on the basis of their ancestral vocations? On the number of stripes that adorned military shoulders? On their ability to extend a business dynasty in a particular way? On their talent for producing movies more memorable, or edgy, than their parents'? I looked at the earnest, sometimes charming expressions these people wore—no, I surmised, they didn't believe it. *Surely,* their searching looks conveyed, *there is more.*

"Like father, like son"; "You're just like your mother"; "It runs in the family"; "You're the spitting image of your grandfather." As charming as these expressions may be, none of them will lead you to an answer to the question *Who am I?* What they are, in fact, are ready sidetracks, incomplete sentences, partial truths to the keener truth that lies within you.

Looking beyond your roots doesn't negate their value. Rather, it places them into the broader context of your life as a whole.

Find a place within yourself to be alone

In the pursuit of separation, everyone needs a refuge. We need a private place where we can be, and test, ourselves without being exposed to the judgments of others. We need a place where we call the shots. Finding such a place carries its own special challenge.

> *Our roots keep us tethered to family, blocking our ability to see ourselves clearly.*

For all the importance we place on imagination, we are consumed by the physical world. It surrounds us, drawing us into its grasp. We live in houses, attend schools, drive to offices to work, or churches and temples to worship. We camp in the woods, swim in the ocean, and take vacations in foreign countries. We *go* from one physical place to another. That is how we live our lives.

Without thinking, we acknowledge just how large and amazing the world around us is. We tell our children to *see the world,* to get to know *what's out there,* to discover other lands and cultures. We are right. The world around us is a giant one. It is full of mystery and excitement. It is worth knowing.

What we often fail to see is that we have a world within us that is at least as large, rich, and mysterious as the one outside. Within this world we have special places to go, which are as exciting as any we might find in the physical world. They are filled with feelings, memories, even answers to nagging questions about life. What makes these places unique, compared to your external destinations, is that you are there by yourself; you are alone. What happens there is entirely up to you. Let your imagination lead.

Imagine a location—a room, a clearing in the woods, someplace you feel comfortable—where you are at its center, surrounded by people you know well. You can see them, but they can't see you.

By comfortable, I mean you feel perfectly safe and at ease there. You have happy memories of this place. You can simply be yourself. Perhaps it is the room you had when you were growing up. Or maybe it is a secret hiding place you ran to when, as a young child, you needed to be alone.

> *The world within us is as large and mysterious as the one outside.*

The people I am referring to are those who have become part of the fabric of your life, and whose presence has added to your sense of security over the course of time. Such people are bound to include members of your immediate, and extended, family. But there are others who probably deserve your attention as well.

When I consider my own life, for example, I am drawn to a variety of seemingly unlikely candidates. One who comes to mind is Miriam, one of my mother's best friends, who died many years ago. Miriam never had children of her own. Because of her love for my mother, I became particularly important to her. Her affection for me was genuine and I felt it at every turn. While Miriam was on the periphery of my life, she occupies an important place in it to this day.

I think as well about Russ. Today, Russ is a dear friend, but our relationship began more than twenty years ago, when he was my boss. In short order, Russ the boss became Russ the mentor. And Russ the mentor eventually evolved into Russ my friend and god-father to my son.

You have such people in your life. Find them. Bring them into this place of comfort. Now imagine these people gradually leaving this place, one at a time, acknowledging one another, but not you, until finally you stand alone.

Why would I do this? you may be wondering. *After all, these are the people who matter most to me and to whom I matter greatly, who make me feel warm and safe inside. Why do I want them to leave me?*

It may seem crazy at first, but allowing them to leave you alone is the challenge at hand. It is exactly because these people are the very ones you've come to count on for comfort that they are the ones you need to have the courage to separate from in order to find your own space.

From this angle, the "refuge" I am talking about is at once comfortable and stark. Being able to live with these two seemingly opposing feelings is an important step on your identity journey.

Finding a place within yourself to be alone will bring you peace no matter how heated your fight for separation may seem at times. You may choose to go there at a moment's notice to steady yourself, and no one but you will know. Spending time in this refuge will help you develop your powers of separation. It will help you build a stronger foundation from which to forge ahead.

Pay special attention to special people

The special relationships we hold with our parents, our children, our mate, if we have one, even teen peers, are fundamental aspects of life. To explore our own identities freely and openly requires that we master these vital relationships, or surely they will master us. By "master" I do not mean control; rather, I mean understand them clearly and deeply. Understand their potential as well as their limitations, their benefits as well as their inevitable shortcomings. You need to make sure you find room within each to be yourself.

Whether you are married or have simply lived with someone

for a time, look upon that person and know that, as much as you may love that individual, he or she is not your "better half." Yes, this popular term of endearment can be a warm, comforting notion that speaks to intimacy and trust. But these people you care about so deeply aren't "half" of you at all. They do not fill in your blanks. You have no blanks. You are whole within yourself.

As a parent, look at your children and honor their distinctiveness—all the things they are that you are not. Love your children, but know that they aren't your salvation. Their lives are not the road to the life you never led as a football hero, a successful entrepreneur, a prima ballerina, or a recognized heart surgeon.

> *Finding a place within yourself to be alone will bring you peace.*

One of the greatest gifts you can give your children is permission to be themselves, not just in what you say but how you say it. It is one thing to tell them that they should find their own way in life. These are noble words and your children need to hear them. But how you convey them gets to the heart of the message.

Said honestly, your words will help your children discover who they are, apart from you. They will decide on their own whether they want to follow in your footsteps or strike a new path. But it can take a bit of courage to mean what you say. Sometimes we encourage our children to find their own way while secretly hoping they'll follow the one we've already set: to be a doctor like we are, or an engineer, or a writer, or one of a number of different vocations that will ensure the family tradition continues.

It is impossible to keep your true wishes hidden from your children. They know you too well. They will sense the message beneath your words.

If you happen to be a teenager, resist the seduction of being popular simply for the sake of being popular. It will drain you of your formative self, and somewhere inside you will know you are faking it. Instead, care for your friends and enjoy their company, but hold your ground. Follow your gut before you follow the leader.

There are obvious reasons to resist the pull of popularity: peer pressure that leads you to indulge in tobacco, alcohol, or drugs; or sexual experimentation that can drastically complicate your life through unwanted pregnancy or disease.

But there are other reasons that aren't at all obvious. In this moment of growth, as you struggle to find your place in the world, you need room—room to find your own integrity as an individual. This "room" lies within you, not outside. It belongs to you and no one else. The more you give in to your friends' desires when those desires are not truly your own, the more you take up precious space inside, the more you crowd out your own integrity, which in the end is what will attract people to you.

> *It is impossible to keep your true wishes from your children.*

As someone's child, whether you are fourteen or forty, work hard to see the person inside your parent. It can take some time before you can finally look into your parent's eyes and see the human being, rather than just "mother" or "father." It isn't easy. In fact, it may be the toughest test of all when it comes to freeing one's self from the invisible bonds that tie us to others' needs.

I recall vividly lying in bed in the recovery room following my first corneal transplant, when I was twenty-seven years old. My mother was seated next to my bed as I woke from the lingering aftereffects of the anesthesia. As her face came into focus, I saw her in a new light. I saw her simply as Anne Ackerman the individual, rather than as *mother.* It was an eerie, unexpected experience. As we talked, and she gazed at what she termed my "new eye," I felt wholly detached from her, from this woman who had brought me into this world. Not bad or good, simply separate.

I never shared this experience with my mother. I wasn't being selfish, nor was I deliberately holding back. That fleeting moment was, for me, a crucial act of growing up, of taking charge of my life and engaging my own integrity. That experience belonged to me—a great, small gift I gave myself that I have treasured ever since.

We are taught, told, and naturally feel the need to regard our parents as always deserving of respect, as in "honor thy mother and father." This way of life has much to recommend it. Most of the time, parents have earned such regard, but their larger-than-life status poses a formidable challenge when it comes to finding our own place to stand on the journey of discovering who we are.

Practice separation every day

Practicing separation daily makes the process easier. It becomes a healthy habit, much like brushing your teeth. As a result, you will feel less anxious. It will seem almost normal. You will come to expect it. With the comfort this routine brings, you may even seek out opportunities to separate, simply as a way to test how adept you have become at managing the process.

Life offers many opportunities to practice the art of separation. They exist in the form of business meetings, both planned and spontaneous; in grocery stores when you run into friends; on trains, buses, or airplanes as you occupy space next to people you know and do not know. As you talk, listen, simply sit, or pass by one another, make the effort to feel the space that exists between you. Consider that space to be a *golden space,* for it testifies to the fact that no matter how much you may care for, and feel close to, those other people, you are remarkably different beings.

A former associate of mine, Tony, practiced separation religiously. For him, it became a way of life that allowed him to build extraordinarily effective relationships with clients and friends.

Tony had a knack for making you feel as though your privacy was important and that he would respect it. Yet he wasn't at all standoffish or distant. In fact, in conversations with Tony, you sensed he was very much with you, in the moment. He was an excellent listener. He responded to your words often by restating what you had said to let you know he had heard you.

In the years we worked together, I watched as my associate built strong and lasting relationships with individuals in the organizations we both served. In more than one instance, Tony's attentiveness led to friendships that survived the work we were doing. One client, a woman in her early forties, wound up joining Tony and some of his friends for weekends at his summer home in New England.

He was a master of social grace, often inviting clients to dinner and taking the conversation in personal directions, where he and his guests spoke about everything but business. Tony was genuine and that made all the difference. He wasn't faking it or feigning interest to be polite, or simply to appeal to the client's good nature. He actually liked getting to know people for who they were—and they responded in kind.

> *Life offers many opportunities to practice the art of separation.*

Tony also had a sixth sense about when to leave people alone. He appreciated boundaries and honored them. If he asked someone to dinner and he or she hesitated, he would instantly demure, suggesting that they pick up their business in the morning. He understood people's need to spend time alone.

Tony practiced separation with artful elegance. As I think about him now, I recall a man who understood the power of separateness, not as a means of keeping people at bay but as a way of caring for them.

As strange as it may seem at first, the need to define one's self as separate from all others precedes our ability to forge genuine relationships. By "genuine" I mean that the people in those relationships have had the courage to find within themselves the strength of character that comes with separateness. As a result, they can give to and take from each other, with no strings attached. Call it freedom: *I am alone; I am free to be who I am.*

> *You are unique within your clan;*
> *complete within yourself.*

You may not know yet who you are in the purest sense of your identity—the special capacities that, when combined, shape your ability to contribute to this world. But know this: you are unique within your clan, complete within yourself. Take from this fact the courage to travel on, knowing that the answer to the question *Who am I?* is there to be found.

This knowledge is the reward of separation. And it is in having had the strength to follow this course that you will realize: *I am alive!*

The following exercises are the first part of the Identity Mapping process. They will help you begin to *know who you are by defining yourself as separate from all others.*

1. Imagine a place—a room, a clearing in the woods, someplace you feel comfortable—where you are standing or sitting at its center, surrounded by people who are carrying on conversations among themselves that you can't hear.

   · In your journal, begin by describing the setting in as much detail as you can. If, for instance, there are chairs present, describe their color. If you are surrounded by trees and bushes, describe their sizes and shapes. Detail your setting. This will make your place all the more memorable in the future.

   · Now identify the people around you, by name. You may include deceased as well as living family members, and others from your past as well as your current life.

   · Imagine these people leaving this place, one at a time. Remember, you can see them, but they can't see you. Write down how being increasingly alone makes you feel as each person departs. Seek to identify your positive as well as negative feelings.

2. Explain briefly how important people in your life are different from you, in terms of their personalities and skills. Avoid passing judgment, such as "She's bad at this,

and I'm good at it." Fill in as many of the following categories as apply.

- My *partner* (spouse, significant other, boyfriend, girlfriend) is different from me in the following ways.

- My *child* is different from me in the following ways. Fill in an answer for each child you have.

- My *mother/father* is different from me in the following ways. Fill in an answer for each of your parents, even if they are deceased.

- My *best friend* is different from me in the following ways. Fill in an answer for your one, or two, best friends.

- My *boss/coworker* is different from me in the following ways. Fill in an answer for those people with whom you must get along in your work in order to succeed.

3. **Find opportunities to acknowledge these important differences. Doing so in a public manner will make them real to you and honor the person in question. Here are some ways for you to consider:**

- Simply tell one or more of these people that you recognize their particular characteristics and how those characteristics affect their lives. Do this in a comfortable setting, when you feel the timing is right.

- Buy small gifts that celebrate the traits that make the people you've named different from you. (I once bought a friend of mine a subscription to a genealogy magazine— a field she loves—even though I have no particular interest in the subject.)

- Use special occasions to let people know that how they are different means something to you. Such occasions may include birthdays and holidays, when sending cards provides an opportunity to express your feelings.

- In business settings, such as meetings, listen actively to the opinions of other people, such as coworkers who may be decidedly different from you, but with whom you must interact. Jot down what you hear as being their most important points. Acknowledge them when it is your turn to speak. Then either restate your position or modify it, based on what you heard.

    Practically speaking, reaching agreement as a group is always important for progress to occur. Keeping that in mind, the goal is for you to assert yourself, based on what you really believe.

THE SECOND QUESTION:

What Makes Me Special?

THE LAW OF INDIVIDUALITY

A person's natural capacities invariably fuse into a
discernible identity that makes that person unique.

*We are not in a position in which we have nothing
to work with. We already have capacities, talents,
direction, missions, callings.*

—ABRAHAM MASLOW

KAREN

It is one thing to know you are alive; it is something else entirely
to live according to who you are. Crossing this divide means
coming to terms with the need to fit in.

Fitting in is something most people seek to do, sometimes consciously, at other times unwittingly. Whether in the office, on the
playing field, or at a dinner party, feeling as though you are a natural part of that environment provides a powerful sense of security.
Call it belonging: "All for one and one for all"; "There is strength
in numbers"; "Membership has its privileges." However you

describe it, fitting in bestows benefits upon the member. Perhaps it is a primal need for community, for protection, even for survival.

Our need to fit in contains an amusing paradox: *being like everyone else makes me special.* For some people, fitting in is all that matters, even if it means denying who you really are.

Such was the case with Karen, first my teacher and then a friend. For all the traits that made her stand out, Karen seemed most concerned with fitting in. She expressed this need in different ways, from her relentless desire to be accepted by her circle of literary friends to her compulsion in restaurants for ordering appetizers and entrées that she felt would "fit in" with what everyone else was having.

Karen was raised in a very modest apartment in New York City: little money, no fancy furniture. What she did have was an expansive view of the Hudson River, which captured her imagination from the time she was a child.

Karen grew up in a musical family. Her father was a voice instructor and professional opera singer. Serious and strict, he taught his daughter the intricacies of his trade. In time, Karen gave her own concerts, not on a grand scale, but for small gatherings and appreciative friends.

> *Fitting in is something most people seek to do.*

Karen majored in French literature in college. She could read, write, and speak French as well as she could English. After she got married, Karen made pin money as a substitute French teacher, which is how I met her.

Between her formal French training and highly disciplined musical roots, Karen appeared to be a person of high culture. Despite her achievements, however, I remember her as being nervous; for some reason, she was uncomfortable in her own skin. As I look back now, her need to fit into the cultured lifestyle she pursued seemed more applied than authentic.

At the school where she substituted, Karen also began teaching English as a second language to young Hispanic and Asian children. Soon she started writing modest books on the subject. As she did, Karen began to change; almost visibly, she began to blossom.

Unlike her sometimes haughty demeanor as a singer, or her a-bit-too-literary persona as a French teacher, Karen shined as brightly as a diamond as she held out her freshly minted books for friends to see. The wonder in her eyes at being published was nearly palpable. Sometimes I would watch her as she tutored youngsters. Her facial muscles would relax noticeably, all signs of self-consciousness vaporizing before me. The lightness of being she radiated in these settings betrayed her love of things far less visible than the trappings her classical upbringing conveyed.

Exactly what did Karen love? The music her father shared with her? Yes, but what I believe she loved most about that music were simply the strains of creativity that pulsed within her. The French she excelled at? Of course, but not as much as the mystery and chance for discovery that foreign cultures came to represent for her.

> *The wonder in her eyes was nearly palpable.*

Karen loved something else, too: the river that beckoned to her as a child from her apartment window. She loved it for the shimmering panorama she remembered, but also for more. She loved it, I sensed, for what it taught her about the power of perspective, about the joy of seeing things from different angles—from other people's points of view.

Karen never saw in herself what I saw in her. Nor did I ever have a chance to share my insights with her before she died. But I do know this: my friend fell headlong into her own happiness in those moments when she wore the mantle of children's author, or touched the chord of learning in some nine-year-old, which in some small way helped bridge a gap in understanding, not just in language. At these times, Karen waded in the waters of those things she loved the most—waters that combined to become the river that formed her identity.

When I think about Karen today, I take comfort in one thing. If my friend had come to know and accept herself in the light of those things she truly loved, rather than the skills she forced herself to embrace and promote, I am confident that her pressing need to fit in would have given way to the honest joys that made her truly special—and genuinely happy.

GETTING TO THE PROMISE OF CLARITY AND CONVICTION

What makes me special? It is a question that takes up residence inside us at an early age, from the time we start forming relationships that draw us away from ourselves and toward the cliques, clubs, companies, and other communities that demand allegiance if we are to be accepted. And yet the more we yield to the pull of acceptance—its alluring comfort—the more the question enters our minds: *What makes me special?* It is as though we have a built-in safety valve that sounds the question whenever we are about to slip out of sight of ourselves. And just before we do, that safety valve goes off. It brings us back, sometimes reluctantly, to the knowledge that we are unique and that, finally—if we want to honor ourselves—we will have no choice but to find out precisely how.

So we sort through the drawers that hold the makings of our

lives, looking for the answer. We open up our jobs to see if what we do for a living defines us. The possibilities in this space are endless: *I am a gifted designer; that is what makes me special. I am a senior banker and am unique in my influence. Being a successful flight attendant makes me, me.* Unfortunately, the answers rarely satisfy. Sometimes they actually cause the question to ring louder in your ears: *What makes me special?*

We open up other drawers as well. We look into our hobbies, into the sports we play, into religion, into the clubs we've joined. We are looking in the wrong places. At least on the surface, the answers aren't there.

Yet despite the frustration that comes from drawing a blank, or from partially formed answers, we continue on. The question lingers, surfacing when we least expect it. This is fortunate, for the answer to the question *What makes me special?* brings with it the promise of clarity and conviction—clarity that you really do have distinctive capacities and what they are, and, in turn, the conviction that there really is a special place for you in the world.

> *There really is a special place for you in the world.*

UNEARTH WHAT YOU LOVE

Realizing the promise of clarity and conviction calls for you to *unearth what you love*—doing the spadework necessary to see what is hidden below the surface of your day-to-day existence to understand those aspects of yourself and life you love the most.

How will you know you've found these treasures? The signs are unmistakable. You will be able to feel your blood pressure drop.

Your endorphins will kick in to produce the emotional equivalent of the well-known runner's high. You will exhale deeply. In that moment, you will be comfortable in your own skin.

Love comes in many forms and with many meanings, all of which find their way into our lives. Sometimes we're casual in our reference to love, as in "I loved that movie" or "I love certain foods." At other moments, our references become much more significant, like when you talk about loving certain people, from parents to friends. The kind of love I am talking about here is different, however. It is about what you need to express in yourself to be happy in your life. It is about unearthing the passions that help define your identity.

Answering the question *What makes me special?* holds great promise. Yet, for all the promise it holds, you may still feel some trepidation in moving ahead. What you uncover, you think, may not be in line with what you do for a living. What you find may not correspond to others' opinions about who you are. Perhaps you're concerned that you won't know how to apply what you learn. Acknowledge your fears and move on. Do not be afraid to look; it is impossible not to love what you find. These treasures are the jewels of your soul.

Suspend disbelief

Most people think they know themselves pretty well. When we're asked to describe ourselves to others, we immediately gravitate to those traits that are most obvious to us. These can range from physical attributes to social strengths, from God-given talents to learned interests. It isn't surprising we take for granted that we know who we are. Whether you're thirteen, thirty, or seventy, you've managed to make your way in the world while realizing what works for you and what doesn't. You've observed your own progress and have come to know yourself well, or so you believe.

Below the surface of your daily life, however, lie aspects of yourself—capacities—you may not be aware of at all. Yet these capacities, like the tectonic plates that determine the movement of the earth's surface, hold the key to understanding what makes you special. The idea that you actually have hidden capacities can be startling. It can lead you to deny such a possibility. The notion that you may not be fully aware of everything there is to know about yourself can even make you feel downright indignant. But that doesn't change the facts.

> *Love is about unearthing the passions that define your identity.*

Unearthing what you love calls for you to suspend disbelief. Allow yourself to consider that there may be things about you that you aren't aware of, invisible characteristics that are essential to your identity. Just because you can't see them doesn't mean they aren't there. Accept that you will not know the answers at first. Realize that there are layers of meaning to the events and activities of your life that have been hidden from view for a long time.

Admitting that you may not at first know all the answers frees you from feeling as though you should know them. *After all,* you may think, *I'm reasonably intelligent and, certainly, old enough to ask the questions. So why aren't the answers obvious to me?* Suspending disbelief will liberate you. Give yourself permission to explore, no strings attached.

Identify what you love doing most

In your hunt for those special joys that inform your identity, let yourself be drawn to those things that stir your heart. They may or may not correspond to your daily activities: your job, hobbies, sports, regular meetings with special friends. Often the best clues to what you love come to you in unlikely places, such as when you're sitting on an airplane at thirty thousand feet, staring out the window. Or when the colors of a particular tree capture and hold your attention, and you forget for the moment where you are. Letting your mind wander can open you to important insights that lie just below the surface of your day.

> *Suspending disbelief will liberate you.*

Don't judge whether your sentiments are correct, or whether the moment is worthy of note. Trust your feelings. Why are you attracted to this experience? What do you get from it? How does it make you feel? Peeling back the layers of your daily routine, one answer after another, is the way to expose those elements that make you special.

As a teenager, I recall walking to school by a very old maple tree that rose above the others. I had known that tree, it seemed, for all time and had always admired its beauty. As usual, one morning I glanced at the tree. As I looked at it, my eyes gravitated to its trunk, which was nearly two feet in diameter. At that moment, everything else around the maple seemed to fade away: the ferns that shaded the roots of the tree and the dozens of saplings around the trunk. My gaze homed in on the bark that blanketed the trunk, and as I moved to within a hand of that maple's skin, I was drawn to the gnarly patterns the bark formed. What had seemed to me until then like no more than a gray-brown sheath had turned into flowing grooves that appeared as small, crisscrossing rivulets, woven together into an intricate fabric, flecked in burnished reds, deep yellows, and mossy greens. In that instant, I found the pattern made by the bark to be more beautiful than the tree itself.

Today, I still remember that moment well. I remember it, however, not so much for how the maple laid bare its miniature world but rather as an awakening within me to what was, and remains, an insatiable curiosity about life in its most graphic and elemental form. My encounter with that tree had been an important clue to what makes me, me, a clue to the answer to the question *What do I love?*

As much as we are used to remembering the external events and experiences that make our lives meaningful, it is equally important—maybe more important—that we identify the internal experiences that give life meaning. Doing so helps make our lives more understandable. Put in other terms, identifying soul-stirring moments is a way to give our lives *inner* structure, just as external events supply the outside structure we rely on to navigate our lives. Consider it part of the basic framework you need in order to know who you are.

Rely only on yourself to define your passions

No one knows more about you than you do. Therefore, the responsibility for your future can only be yours. Taking this responsibility to heart will lead you to invest more of yourself in whatever you do. You will become more discerning in your choices. You will sleep more soundly under the blanket of your own integrity.

Yet gathering other people's views about you—their perceptions of your talents, skills, and aptitudes—makes perfect sense in your efforts to guide yourself forward. Listening to others is a useful way for you to gauge how you feel about yourself. You are not seeking answers. What you are seeking are *clues,* vital clues about who you are, and who you are not.

Unfortunately, my friend Karen listened too hard to what other people had to say. I recall many conversations with Karen where she would recount the times she was "told" what she was good at by her father: Karen was a singer; she was a scholar; she was cultured. Karen started receiving these messages from the time she was a child. Every time she asked close friends to tell her what they saw, they would invariably defer to what they knew her father and, to a lesser degree, her mother had told her—all of her friends but one.

> *Identifying soul-stirring moments gives your life inner structure.*

When Karen arrived at college, she met a woman named Gina. In contrast to Karen's shy and retiring personality, Gina had an unmistakable independent streak. She was outspoken and tough. She laughed a lot. Karen and Gina became fast friends, resulting, I imagine, from just how different they were.

It was Gina who saw through Karen's programmed exterior and into her heart. She cajoled Karen, pressing her to think for herself. They took classes together, including history and creative writing. It was in these moments that Gina witnessed Karen's "other side"—her love for learning about other cultures and her flair for writing in lively, memorable prose.

Gina never hesitated to point out these traits to her friend. While Karen was flattered and genuinely delighted by her friend's observations, she was also a bit nervous. Such characteristics didn't fit her self-image. They weren't in line with what she had been told about herself by her parents and others since the time she was very young. But Gina's observations were true.

It would take another twenty years before Karen would respond to the vital clues her friend had supplied, taking them to heart and reshaping her life around the teaching and writing she loved.

With the best of intentions, other people form their own views about what you are really good at and, as a result, what you should and shouldn't be doing with your life. For example, our early attraction to career paths that our parents, or their lives, suggest should come as no surprise. It is only natural to look to our parents for clues about our own identity. And, in fact, there usually is something to be learned, something informing that springs from the bonds that biology provides. That said, however, these bonds have their limits; they are a beginning, not an end. Your parents contribute to your identity by combining the seeds of innumerable generations into the formation of a unique being—you. Beyond that, their job is to get to know, and nurture, the individual you are.

Unearthing what you love takes perseverance. What you learn at first may only be the tip of the iceberg. In my case, when I finally confronted the large maple tree, it took a while before I understood what it was about that tree that was really calling to me—the world of colors, angles, and crevices that was buried in its bark. There was more to that maple than what had first met my eye. There is always more in front of you than you initially see.

> *Your parents' job is to get to know, and nurture, the individual you are.*

You will know what makes you special when you recognize in yourself strengths and passions that are deeply comforting and yet seem fresh and new. There may be no more than three or four of these capacities, but they are all you need. They form the "inner structure" of your life that I noted earlier. They are the foundation of your identity.

Building this foundation is the reward for unearthing what you love. It is yours alone to stand on, a place to realize and then assert: *I am unique.*

EXERCISES IN DISCOVERY

The following exercises are the second part of the Identity Mapping process. They will help you *learn what makes you special by unearthing what you love*. These exercises are designed to respond, directly and indirectly, to the different steps presented in this chapter. In some instances, they may go beyond the examples the chapter provides.

1. **Name the things you "love"—and love to do** (for example, skiing, mountain climbing, cooking, singing, being in nature, riding horses, dancing, gardening, stamp collecting). What they are and how many there are isn't important. List them next to one another.

2. **For each activity you've named, identify the *whys*.** Why is each significant to you? What feelings does each elicit? For each of these answers, ask "why" again. Why is that particular feeling important to you? (It's all about the *whys*!) Create a thorough list of answers under each activity or experience.

3. **Ask for help.** Ask people whose opinions you respect to help you identify the *whys*. It is easy to get distracted from your challenge, or to let yourself off the hook too quickly. There is a well of unconscious knowledge inside you, waiting to be tapped. Find someone to act as your partner or coach to help you stay focused.

4. **Find the similarities.** Look at each list and circle words that are the same, or similar in meaning, from column to column. Even consider words, or terms—key words—that may allude

to a similar idea but are differently stated (for example, *won-derment, discovery, mystery*). Circle them, too.

5. **Name the themes.** Draw a line connecting the various key words you've identified, from one list to the next. (Not all lists will necessarily contain a key word.) Now define the theme that best captures the idea represented by that particular connection. It may be the dominant word across columns, or another word that is implied by the key words, or terms, you've circled. Write the theme in block letters on the appropriate line of the diagram you've created. It is these themes that help illuminate what you love.

THE THIRD QUESTION:

Is There a Pattern to My Life?

THE LAW OF CONSTANCY

Identity is fixed, transcending time and place, while
its manifestations are constantly changing.

———

Life is the act of becoming. Life is transitional.
That's what I am engaged in:
to continue to become more of me. . . .

—MARTIN BUBER

GEORGE

Since the time we are children, patterns capture our imaginations and influence our lives. As infants, we are mesmerized by the patterns that light and color form. Later, we amuse ourselves with games of connect the dots: we find the animals—birds, elephants, giraffes—or the landscapes, or people hidden in the pages of books that contain visual mysteries.

As time passes and life becomes more serious, the decisions we make—the school courses we take; the jobs, sports, and hobbies we choose—become the "dots" of our lives. If we are aware of the pattern they are forming, and decode its message, we are indeed fortunate. We are then in a position to understand a bit more about who we are, what we love, and where we might go in our careers and even our relationships.

Most people aren't so fortunate. They don't see the pattern hidden in the many experiences of their lives. Or they believe that the only pattern to be found will be a negative one, such as a string of bad marriages, or a tendency to overeat, overspend, or drink too much. Such negative patterns of behavior may exist, but they say nothing about who you are.

In truth, many people believe that there is no pattern at all, that their lives are composed simply of random events, where they move from job to job, or place to place, as opportunity knocks, or as fate would have it. For them, choice and free will rule. These are people destined to go through life having missed the big picture—their own.

Other people, however, are genuinely lucky; they figure it out just in time. My friend George was one of them.

By the time George was twenty-nine, he had held three jobs. One job, as the business manager for a local arts organization, he quit after a year. The other two he was fired from: a job as a buying assistant for a retailer that lasted six months, and one as a project director for a market research firm.

> *Many people don't see the pattern hidden in the experiences of their lives.*

George was frightened. My friend was lost. At my urging, he decided to take stock of what had been his life so far. Neither one of us knew exactly what this meant, nor where this might lead. But we agreed that there was no harm in him going through the exercise.

As George described it to me several weeks later, what he called his epiphany occurred in a run-of-the-mill coffee shop in the middle of San Francisco. He was very early for a job interview as a sales account executive for a shoe company and had time to kill.

As he sat in his booth, my friend tore a piece of paper from his writing pad. Over the next hour or so, he jotted down experiences that were particularly memorable, the ones he felt had been the milestones of his still young life.

Reaching back in time, George began with how he had sculpted the figures of bears out of clay as a child in second grade. His recollections went on to include his love of black-and-white photography as a teenager, and writing awards he had won in high school for essays and poetry. Quickly, he counted among his memories his love of classical and flamenco guitar, which he had studied and played since he was eight years old. Further, George recalled his passion for the martial arts—particularly the intricate, choreographed forms he had learned—which blossomed in college. He even acknowledged his deep attraction to the world of research, a world from which he had just been separated, owing to a company-wide layoff.

Sensing that his list was complete, George began drawing small icons of the different milestones he had managed to recall. His recent research job, for example, took the form of a treasure chest, to suggest the notion of discovery. Not surprisingly, he rendered photography as a camera and sketched the figure of a man in a karate uniform to capture his interest in the martial arts. He drew a guitar to symbolize music and a quill to symbolize writing. The sculptures he created in second grade he executed as closely as he could to the real thing: a piece of driftwood with two bears perched on a branch.

Six vital, if seemingly unrelated, aspects of George's life lay before him. He took his pencil and traced a line connecting the primitive icons. His drawing formed a ragged oval. As George tells it, he stared at that oval for what seemed to him like a day. And then, picking up his pencil, he wrote in the center of the oval the letters *c r e a t i v i t y.*

George had put his finger on the one thing he realized was the constant in his life, the common thread that stitched together innumerable strands into a single, revealing tapestry. These seemingly random experiences highlighted an unmistakable, undeniable love for all things creative—indeed, for the act of creation itself.

George's mind raced. As he explained to me later, it was no wonder he had failed at his job in retailing and as an arts administrator. Neither one had called upon his creative drive. Creativity, he recalled being told by his respective employers, was for the clothing designers and the performing artists, not for business managers.

George never went to his interview with the shoe company. He called and canceled the appointment. For the rest of the day and, I imagine, for many days and weeks after that, George let what he had learned about himself wash over and through him.

Today, twenty years later, George is a partner in a research firm, which he helped found. The company is considered to be one of the most inventive organizations on the West Coast.

> *He loved all things creative; indeed,*
> *the act of creation itself.*

GETTING TO THE PROMISE OF ORDER AND MEANING

For all we can learn about ourselves from uncovering the patterns our lives contain, asking what that pattern is still rattles us. It makes us uncomfortable. On one hand, we are likely to see things about ourselves that are energizing and powerful. Simply finding this pattern—the one that is well established at sixty or just forming at sixteen—can provide a reliable guide for improving the quality of our lives.

On the other hand, what we fear we may discover, once we've figured out the mystery, is that we've made big, irreversibly damaging mistakes, along with the many small ones that dot everyone's life. So, we don't look. We behave like the ostrich and stick our heads in the sand. We'd rather not know.

What we fail to realize by taking this course is that no matter how hard we try, we can't wish the pattern away, or make it different from what it is. We also don't realize that at least parts of both outcomes are likely—the "good" one and the "bad" one. Finding the pattern your life contains means separating the wheat from the chaff. And we all have both. In truth, the pattern you are looking for is neither positive nor negative. It simply *is*. What you learn about yourself from your mistakes as well as your triumphs is what counts, not the experiences themselves.

To find the pattern your life contains is to find the path that has been right for you all along. Making this path visible can lead to many things: changing jobs or schools, marrying, divorcing, making new friends and dropping others, converting to another religion, or simply reaffirming and celebrating the course you have taken to date.

> *Find the pattern of your life and you will find the path that has been right for you all along.*

In this process, it is comforting to know that change doesn't necessarily mean leaving important parts of yourself behind. And sometimes what you may see as change isn't really change at all; it is simply another way of expressing who you already are.

Embracing your identity allows you to live comfortably at the intersection where change and constancy inevitably meet. Here, you are in a position to "change" from a changeless foundation. You can experiment with confidence, test yourself, stretch and reach out, knowing that your identity will keep you from following false trails.

In finding your pattern, you are seeking not only to discover but to create the story of your life in a way that will help ensure a "happy ending."

Answering the question *Is there a pattern to my life?* carries with it the exhilarating promise that your life has order and meaning. Put plainly, that you haven't wasted your time, that your efforts—your successes as well as your failures—add up to something essential and telling about who you are.

One of the most disconcerting feelings you can have is feeling adrift, as though you've lost your bearings in stormy seas, while hidden rocks make navigation treacherous. I have met many people whose lives appear perfectly neat and orderly on the surface, but underneath their waters are roiling. Their résumé reveals a history of too many jobs. Or the job they're in seems endless and empty beyond the paycheck they get every week. Their relationship with their spouse, or partner, is, in their own words, "up and down." Or they watch in envy as their children fashion lives that seem to hold greater promise than, they believe, their own ever will.

Order seems to have eluded them: that feeling that things fit together correctly, that the pieces of their lives blend with a sense of harmony, no matter how dramatically different those pieces may be.

Without order, it is impossible to find meaning in life. Some people assert that they don't care whether life has meaning. They claim to be happy with their money, or simply with the time they have. The notion of "meaning" is too grand, too elusive, for them. Too much time has gone by. Secretly, they may believe that hoping to find meaning is a recipe for finding nothing but disappointment. They are wrong.

> *Without order, it is impossible to find meaning in life.*

Like order, meaning is inherent in everyone's life. Meaning isn't some highfalutin idea that applies only to gurus who meditate while sitting on mountaintops. In fact, the idea that your life has meaning is exquisitely simple. It refers to your intrinsic worth as a human being—the fact that you have value in this world simply as a result of being here. Finding the pattern of your life reveals both its order and its meaning. Once discovered, you will be able to say, *Now I see.*

MAKE THE CONNECTIONS THAT EXPLAIN PAST EVENTS AND FORESHADOW YOUR FUTURE

The pattern your life contains is visible only if you know what to look for and how to look. What does it take? The way to find the pattern in your life is by *making the connections that explain past events and foreshadow your future.*

A helpful analogy to keep in mind as you search for your pattern is the constellations that turn the night sky into stories. On their own, the millions of stars that dot the sky are impressive in their own right. They evoke feelings ranging from humility—how small we are compared to the vastness of space—to romance. In a similar vein, that ocean of experiences that makes up our lives is equally impressive—rich, varied, and vast.

Link certain stars, however, and suddenly you find the constellation buried in their midst. Each constellation contains a pattern with a theme all its own. Suddenly, the night sky, seemingly an endless tapestry of random stars, takes on greater order and meaning.

Consider, for instance, the pattern known as Orion, the hunter. The constellation Orion was used by people ages ago to predict the seasons. A midnight rising of Orion meant that the grapes were ready to be harvested. A morning rising meant that summer was beginning, and an evening rising signaled that winter was here. Orion may have been looked upon as a hunter with a nose for seasonal change—that may have been his most obvious role—but the driving theme underlying his story is all about *guidance*.

That is what you are looking for: the theme that is a part of your identity story, which will help you put your life into perspective as you look back and as you look forward.

Consider your most memorable achievements

In finding the pattern to your life, let your achievements light the way. Your achievements are about giving. They reveal insights about what matters to you, what you love, and where your passions truly lie. They are vital indicators of how you can make a difference in the world. As much as the idea is often greeted with cynicism, and sometimes even denial, the desire to be a productive member of society is hardwired into everyone.

Achievements are something we all need to experience in order to feel alive, even human. They make us feel good about ourselves in ways that can last a lifetime. Your achievements may be small or large, glamorous or mundane. They can include recent job successes, childhood accomplishments that engender warm feelings, important sports victories, longstanding hobbies, awards won, poems published, caring for a sick family member or friend, community activities, or any number of experiences that simply make you feel good about yourself. Consider achievements from different ages, so that you paint a comprehensive picture of your life.

Just as you consider experiences from different times in your life, also seek variety. Your world may revolve around sports, or business, or some other field that provides you with a center of gravity. Certainly, it is important to consider accomplishments in this particular field, but don't limit your search to it. Force yourself to look beyond the bounds of this special world and identify achievements—victories—in other parts of your life as well. Keep in mind that you are seeking to find the pattern that reveals who you are as a complete person.

Take stock of your failures

In almost every field of endeavor, we are told that we learn more from our mistakes than from our successes. Yet it can be painful to face them, especially those that have cost us dearly: ill-fated jobs, poor choices of partners or friends, expensive country clubs or popular fraternities or sororities where we find we just don't fit in.

Let your achievements light the way.

But your failures often hold precious clues to the pattern you seek. The feelings of personal failure my friend George harbored following the humiliation of losing two jobs in a row evaporated when he finally came to see how neither line of work let him express his creativity, which was central to his happiness. In an instant, my friend saw the "logic" of his own failure. He understood why he was fired—he shouldn't have been in either position in the first place. As George came to terms with this experience, he breathed easier. He forgave himself for his missteps. He even felt lucky that someone had "helped" him come to terms with what really mattered to him, and what did not.

None of us is perfect. Sometimes, even with the noblest of intentions—income, friendship, social standing, family acceptance—we pursue wrong paths. On the other side of the coin we call failure, however, is information we can use to set ourselves right—illuminating knowledge about what we really are good at that points the way forward.

Connect the dots

As much as we divide our days into parts to help keep things manageable—work or school, family, friends, social occasions, hobbies, and sports—we are, in the end, complete, undivided individuals. Our value as people can be measured only by the totality of our lives. Forcing yourself to connect the dots your life contains is a way to honor the wholeness of your being.

Together, your achievements, both great and small, coupled with the liberating insights your failures yield hold the key to finding the pattern of your life. Imagine these experiences organized into groups. These groups can revolve around virtually any theme that describes, in broad terms, what you love: nature, discovery, creativity, community. What they *cannot* do is revolve around specific professions: for instance, business, law, sports, medicine, carpentry, or cooking. The pattern of your life reveals important insights into who you are. Only after you have drawn those insights will you be in a position to consider what they may mean in terms of your career path, or vocation.

Making the connections that explain past events and foreshadow your future is at once challenging and exhilarating. You are your own detective. Put together the pieces of your puzzle and you will discover the secret it holds. What is this secret? It is that, for all the turns you make in your life, the wrong ones as well as the right ones, who you are at the core of your being has never changed, always remains secure, and is ready to be tapped at any age.

> *Your failures often hold clues to the pattern you seek.*

Having uncovered the pattern your life contains, you will realize this simple truth: *I am immutable, even as I grow and evolve.*

The following exercises are the third part of the Identity Mapping process. They will help you *find the pattern to your life by making the connections that explain past events and foreshadow your future.* These exercises are designed to respond, directly and indirectly, to the different steps presented in this chapter. In some instances, they may go beyond the examples the chapter provides.

1. **Identify your most memorable achievements.** These can be specific experiences or areas of experience (for example, winning a specific creative writing award, or, say, short-story writing, generally). Include all the years from your child-hood until now. Don't force the process; trust your instincts. Make sure your achievements are varied, reflecting different aspects of your life. To help crystallize which ones are truly most important, write down why each achievement was, or is, significant to you.

2. **Describe one or two memorable failures** and what you learned about yourself from them that was positive—such as a hidden strength or talent that, in other circumstances, has actually contributed to an important achievement.

3. **For each achievement create a simple icon, or symbol,** that expresses it. (The reason for using geometric shapes is that we are all visual by nature, and shapes make it easier for us to identify with the idea we're trying to express.) Array these icons in a circle or other geometric form. Now draw a line connecting them.

4. **Write down the theme that emerges.** Identify one over-arching theme that ties all of these achievements together and write it in the middle of the form you've drawn.

5. **Based on this theme, record the "story" that is hidden in the pattern of your life** and that helps explain past events and foreshadows your future. Write down the essence of that story in one sentence.

THE FOURTH QUESTION:

Where Am I Going?

THE LAW OF WILL

Every individual is compelled to create value in
accordance with his or her identity.

---

*Whatever you are by nature, keep to it. Never desert your
own line of talent. Be what nature intended you for
and you will succeed; be anything less and you
will be ten thousand times worse than nothing.*

—SYDNEY SMITH

TERRY

W e are all tempted at times to do it: to walk away from a
challenge when the task seems too great, the pressure is
too much, or the odds of succeeding seem to be stacked against us.

Sometimes the challenge you face is mostly physical, like running five miles or losing five pounds. Sometimes the task is equally
emotional, such as when you must care for a sick family member
by yourself and there is no end in sight and your patience is wearing thin. At other times the challenge can be downright unsettling,

like when you feel the stirrings of change inside—the need to change what you are doing with your life and how you are living it—but you aren't exactly sure what those stirrings mean.

Some people do it then: they give up. They tell themselves the task is too hard. It isn't worth the effort. Or they simply can't do it alone. So they quit running and eat cake. Despite deep misgivings, they put their family charge into a nursing home. They ignore the churnings inside that have surfaced without warning.

Some people walk away, but others don't. For them, the fight is worth it. They are blessed. Especially those who are stirred to change within themselves, even when they are not sure where they are heading. In the midst of doubt they decide to stay the course. Somehow they know that where they are going will be better than where they have been. They are fortunate to have the courage to live with the uncertainty that personal transformation inevitably brings. My friend Terry was blessed in this way.

For all intents and purposes, Terry was a successful person; she lived a good life. Terry had been married to the same man for more than twenty years. She was mother to a teenage son, who held his own in school, loved team sports, and in social situations showed an uncanny knack for leading others. Further, Terry had risen through the financial ranks of a well-respected health-care organization, where she had become a vice president.

> *Have the courage to live with the uncertainty personal transformation brings.*

Yet my friend was less than happy. In fact, despite her seemingly "good life," she wasn't really happy at all. Much of Terry's drive to succeed had been trained into her as a child. With the best of intentions, her parents had insisted she follow a career in business.

Despite Terry's decidedly different interests and skills, no other paths were acceptable. Her mother and father believed that a traditional career was the only way to ensure that their daughter would be able to live independently, no matter what fate might bring.

Now, decades later, Terry had decided to take stock of her life. A gnawing pain had taken root at the base of her stomach and become too much to bear. The need to free herself from it became her unspoken obsession.

With my encouragement and guidance, Terry did the hard work of discovery; she unearthed what she loved. She started by identifying those things in life she was drawn to. These included horses, dance, history, travel, gardening, and nature. After examining why each was so important, my friend began to understand the special capacities these interests represented: a passion for movement, growth, and discovery; a love of freedom and purity. On the surface, few of these traits seemed to relate to financial management, which is where she had invested her energy for more than two decades.

In the months that followed, Terry's emotions ran from elation to despair. She had come to see herself more clearly as the individual she was. Yet she still had no firm idea of what to do with her newfound knowledge. Quit her job and reassess everything? Stay where she was and pretend that what she had discovered had no bearing on what she did every day?

Terry admitted to me one evening that her mounting confusion was taking a toll on her family: her emotional ups and downs were causing her to lash out at her husband, and sometimes even her son. Had her efforts been worth it, she wondered? For all she had learned about herself, for all the promise she felt about the possibility of a fuller, more authentic life, Terry felt unsure about what to do next.

Weeks later, I received a call from my friend early on a Sunday morning. With remarkable calm in her voice, she told me that she had had a dream the night before, which she wanted to share with me. We met that afternoon. Terry pulled a crumpled piece of paper from her pocket on which she had scribbled her dream. The following is what she described.

It was early in the morning. She stood on the edge of a bank at the end of a spit of land that pointed out over the horizon. Terry stared across the water to the opposite shore. It was, she guessed, at least a half mile off and was covered with dazzling vegetation.

Despite the distance, she could make out the forms of enormous trees blossoming with fruits, vegetables, and flowers, many of which she recognized. But others she had apparently never seen before. The combined effect was striking. As she took in this sight, she felt as though two seasons, autumn and spring, had somehow fused into one, producing a new variety of plant life. She strained to get a better look, squinting into the distance to make sense of this startling new form of nature.

Terry paused for a moment from recounting her dream. Averting my gaze, she stared out the window. After several seconds, she continued. Looking at me intently, she told me how she longed to reach that other shore. She felt as though she were being pulled toward it. For some unexplainable reason, she sensed she belonged there. She wanted to partake in the extraordinary bounty that covered the land, but she couldn't move. All she could do was stand there, for what seemed like hours.

Terry felt paralyzed yet alive with desire. She realized she had no clear way to make the voyage across the water. Yet, the more time passed, the more she wanted to get to that other side, where, she was now convinced, she was meant to be.

> *Two seasons, autumn and spring, had somehow fused into one.*

Terry explained that the tension she had felt in her dream became unbearable. Her heart raced. She began to hyperventilate. Suddenly, she felt dizzy, her knees buckled, and the light of morning went dark. That is when she woke up.

Staring at her, I now understood why my friend's voice had been so calm when she called me that morning. Terry's dream had made her will clear: *there was no going back.* The prospect of abandoning the beauty and power she had found in herself was unthinkable. The only chance she would have in life to express herself fully would be if she marched forward, no matter how long it might take to "reach the other shore."

GETTING TO THE PROMISE
OF FAITH AND FORTITUDE

Where am I going? It is a question we ask ourselves more often than we may care to admit. Most people ask it out of frustration: they don't really know, as much as they would like to. We ask ourselves the question while walking down supermarket aisles, or while chitchatting at cocktail parties, or driving to work, or changing diapers. As we do, we are living two separate lives: the one that is easily observed by others—the store cashier, an engaging stranger, the person in the car next to us, the child in our arms—and the secret one only we know about, where the question bubbles up. Reconciling these two lives is a dream many people share.

The Law of Will takes each of us to the edge of an untenable place in our lives. Having discovered what makes you special, you awaken, perhaps for the first time, to the idea that your future is in some way knowable. You have unearthed the seeds of your identity, those special characteristics that inform who you are. You have discovered the pattern of your life. Instinctively, you are compelled to bring these powerful traits to bear, whatever it takes.

89

Even if it isn't well lit, you sense the path is right before your eyes, but you don't yet know how to move forward. Consider this experience the half-birth of your identity: you have gained enough knowledge about yourself to be encouraged, but not enough to know for certain where this knowledge may lead you.

It is in the midst of this self-imposed paralysis that you are tested: do you abandon, or ignore, what you have learned about yourself and simply go on as before? Or do you accept your unfinished state and hold on to the belief that there is more to come, if you only stay the course?

For all the exasperation it produces, addressing the question *Where am I going?* also brings with it the promise of faith and fortitude: faith in the process of discovery, in the power of the code you seek to decipher, in yourself. It is in the crucible in which this faith is forged that you will find the strength you need to shore yourself up against the maddening lack of visibility that clouds your future.

> *In the midst of this self-imposed paralysis,*
> *you are tested.*

You can't simply pull a switch or press a button inside yourself and find the kind of faith I am referring to. You have to cross the divide—the one that separates your uncertain, diffident self from your gritty, determined self. The divide that may seem insurmountable at times, as though attempting to cross it can bring only trouble.

I have crossed this divide more than once. One of the most memorable experiences occurred when I was in my late thirties and was running a small consulting firm called Identica. Identica was dedicated to bringing identity-based thinking to organizations. I had left my former employer—a well-known, highly successful consulting concern—because I needed room to test and develop my own ideas of what identity was all about and how it affected institutions and people.

Based largely on the work I had done only over the past few years, my ideas were formative at best. But they tugged at me. The more I applied them in my job, the more I saw their potential. I needed space. I needed room to run.

It was a rocky road. In the four years Identica existed, we succeeded in winning important assignments with the likes of Alcoa, the world's largest aluminum company, and Upjohn, then one of America's leading pharmaceutical makers. For me, these weren't simply business opportunities; they were the laboratories in which I ran my identity experiments. These engagements were the foundation for discovering how human identity and organizational identity operated according to what, years later, I realized were the same set of natural laws—the Laws of Identity.

Our fourth year brought us an offer to be acquired by a British firm that was especially interested in how Identica did things: our way was different and deeper than others, and produced results that were more grounded in the fabric of the client's business. Typically, for instance, the implications of our work touched not only how the client communicated and presented itself but how it developed leaders, trained employees, and recruited new talent.

After several months, we agreed to be bought. One week before the deal was scheduled to be finalized, I received a phone call from the finance director of the British company. He told me that their stock had plummeted and that they could no longer afford to make the purchase: the deal was off.

We never recovered from the shock of that decision. We had placed our bet on being part of a larger, better-funded concern—

a bet we had now lost. Identica did not survive, and I was out of work. I had invested four years of my life in the firm and in crafting what were now the proven underpinnings of my theory on identity. But I needed a job.

Over the following months, I struggled to keep my bearings, to not simply abandon what I had learned and take the first position that was offered to me in my field. I knew I was onto something important, something that deserved to live on. To just walk away from my identity work was inconceivable. It would have been as though I were turning my back on myself.

Those were bleak times for me. One moment I was scared about my lack of income. In the next, I was elated with what I had managed to achieve under the banner of Identica. At other times, I became angry with myself for seemingly having wasted four years of my life, selfishly focusing on creating a consulting approach that might never be widely embraced by people. I went from feeling insecure to emboldened, and back again, dozens of times a day. Fatigue became my companion.

Nearly three months after Identica had been dissolved, I was going to bed and it hit me. I suddenly felt the weight of uncertainty and fear dissolve in my gut, like a mountain of snow melting quickly in the heat of a March sun, to reveal the earth beneath it. I would not, could not, walk away from what I had created. I would find a way to take it with me, no matter what. In that moment, I found the faith in myself I needed to move ahead. I had crossed the divide.

> *Identica did not survive, and I was out of work.*

A few weeks later, I accepted an offer to rejoin my former firm, where I spent the next eight years applying what I had learned, sharpening my ideas and practices, and helping my clients succeed in the process.

How do you find the faith I am speaking of? The way to realize the promise of faith and the fortitude it brings is by *committing to the path revealed in what you have learned so far.*

COMMIT YOURSELF TO THE PATH
REVEALED IN WHAT YOU'VE
LEARNED SO FAR

Commitment requires bravery. We choose a mate, someone we feel, with all our heart, is right for us, yet we really don't know until after we've moved in with him or her, or said "I do"—until we've committed ourselves. Without knowing it, bravery has seeped into our bones. The same holds for the jobs we choose, or the colleges we pick, or the opinions we offer publicly, which may or may not be well received by others. We throw ourselves into the unknown, based on what we've learned or experienced so far.

Commitment thrives on uncertainty. Uncertainty teases out of us a sense of resolve we didn't even know we had. It brings us face-to-face with risk and the edgy discomfort that risk brings. But commitment is what the Law of Will demands of us.

Let the future go

Focusing on the future can either be a healthy, empowering exercise or an utter waste of time. Most people harbor dreams of how they would like their lives to be. They envision everything from businesses they'd like to start and sports teams they'd like to play for to how they'd like their marriages to work, or their relationships with their children to be. Keeping these dreams intact and revisiting them periodically enables people to stay focused in a healthy way. Such dreams keep their spirits alive and can lead them to make constructive decisions about what they do with the time they have.

Other people want to know now how the future will actually turn out. They're hell-bent on trying to manage their futures, as though they were automobiles to be steered in whatever direction they choose. They pour themselves into this exercise in earnest. For these people, ambiguity is painful. Not knowing is almost worse than failing to achieve the goals they've set for themselves. This approach to the future takes you nowhere.

Attempting to figure out exactly where you are going in life brings with it equal amounts of wonder and aggravation. As much as it is impossible to predict your future, attempting to do so can be irresistible. We are cajoled by well-meaning family members, teachers, and friends to try to set a course for ourselves we can count on. Having discovered talents, skills, and passions we never knew we had, we push ourselves to figure out how we can best use these capacities to shape a life worth living.

But all we can really do—all that is really worth doing—is to figure out how to use today the special strengths that begin to reveal what our value-creating potential is. We have control over what we do now and how we do it. Taken one at a time, each of our days becomes our future. That is how the future is formed.

In practical terms, it is also important to realize that your ability to know your future is constrained by old ways of thinking that have taken root over many years. "Letting go" of your future, then, is a symbolic act, a process through which you can begin to release yourself from old ways of thinking and behaving that may have been holding you back.

The answer to the question *Where am I going?* isn't simply *I don't know;* the correct answer is *I don't know, but that is all right.* There is no need to know everything about tomorrow all at once. There is no need for crystal balls. Accepting uncertainty is a measure of your maturity. It is an act of trust in yourself, a crucial milestone you must reach in order to move forward.

Embrace your strengths

There is a saying that less is more. Sometimes what you already possess is enough, at least for the moment. Whatever they may be, your special capacities deserve recognition. More than likely, these strengths, which have been with you forever, represent new information. In this sense, they are fragile and need to be cultivated. They need to take root in your life.

> *Attempting to figure out where you're going in life brings with it both wonder and aggravation.*

The more you can make these strengths part of your daily routine, the more they will begin to lead you forward. Using language that reinforces your distinctive capacities will influence what you say to others and how you say it. Think about how your particular passions might change how you do your job, and follow the course this suggests.

In the weeks following her dream, my friend Terry started creating personal key words based on the strengths she had discovered about herself. *Freedom, growth, discovery,* and *movement* became part of her daily lexicon. Gradually, she brought these words into discussions with her boss at the health-care company where she worked. One day, Terry proposed that the main mission for the finance department she helped run should change. Rather than financial stability, she suggested that their mission should be ensuring that the company had the freedom to grow. Terry argued that although this mission called for financial stability, it also called for more: from now on, the finance department would define its true value by how well its actions helped the company develop and apply the special strengths that enabled it to succeed.

Two weeks after considering her proposal, Terry's boss accepted it. What made Terry happy, however, wasn't her professional victory; it was finding a way to bring the best of herself to bear in her workplace. Terry had found a meaningful way to bring to life her passion for movement, growth, and discovery, and the love of freedom that made her who she was.

Acknowledge that your life will change

The Law of Will asserts that at the core of our beings, we all want to create something of value that flows naturally from who we are. The desire to create is part of what makes us human. Knowing what that creation is, whether it is large or small, will in time reveal the answer to the question *Where am I going?*

You have reached a point in deciphering your identity code that tests your will severely. You cannot fast-forward the movie of your life to see how it will turn out. What you can do is accept the idea that what you do in the future, based on what you've learned about yourself so far, is likely to be different than what you do today. If not *what* you do, by way of career or vocation, then *how* you do it.

Be patient. Welcome change. Acknowledging the prospect that you will live differently tomorrow will open you up to new possibilities. It will free you from the pressure you feel to have the answers now. Much like opening a window, it will allow the fresh breezes you seek to sweep into your life.

You will know you have deciphered this portion of your identity code when you feel the kind of gnawing hunger that comes when you haven't eaten for a while. When your thoughts are colored by images of the nourishment you crave but can't have. The fourth law is designed to be that way. It is designed to bring you to a place of visceral discomfort, to test your resolve. Committing to the path revealed in what you've learned so far takes determination. It takes willpower.

The desire to create is part of what makes us human.

In surviving the trials of uncertainty, you will find the faith and fortitude you need to travel on. You will affirm one thing above all: *to live, I must express myself fully.*

EXERCISES IN COMMITMENT

The following exercises are the fourth part of the Identity Mapping process. They will help you *understand where you are going by committing to the path revealed in what you've learned so far.* These exercises are designed to respond, directly and indirectly, to the different steps presented in this chapter. In some instances, they may go beyond the examples the chapter provides.

1. **Identify at least three different settings where you can start to apply your special capacities,** including those things you love and the pattern your life reveals. Consider such environments as your work, the classroom, your home, and job interviews, even college applications that call for you to write an essay about yourself.

2. **Develop a vocabulary all your own.** Create a list of words and phrases that build upon each of your special capacities and are meaningful to you.

3. **Begin to use your vocabulary in conversations and writing.** "Bake" its content into how you communicate with others. Use it when people need to know who you are, what you believe in, and how you approach solving problems and meeting challenges.

4. **Write down how your unique capacities might change the way you approach your current job, or, if you are a student, your studies.** Identify at least three concrete possibilities. Find opportunities to apply your ideas and make at least one happen in the next month. After you're done, write down

the "before and after" situation, describing how the application of your capacities affected the outcome.

5. **Identify which aspects of your life are likely to change the most** if you stay the course prescribed by what you've learned so far about yourself. State why you picked the relationships, or experiences, you did. Then record how you believe each of these might change. Use your imagination. Be as specific as possible.

THE FIFTH QUESTION:

What Is My Gift?

THE LAW OF POSSIBILITY

Identity foreshadows potential.

We are each gifted in a unique and important way.
It is our privilege and our adventure
to discover our own special light.

—Mary Dunbar

DIANE

Many people are happy just getting along. They're happy making ends meet and avoiding problems that might upend their lives. They are content having enough money and time to enjoy a few of life's pleasures. At least, that's what they say.

The idea that each of us is born with a particular gift that informs what we might do with our lives scares people. The thought that you may actually have something akin to a purpose can be unnerving. The reasons are many.

What if you fail to figure it out in time, even though you know it's there? What price will you pay that you aren't even aware of?

Or, perhaps, worse: what if you know what your gift is, but never find the courage, or way, to give it?

Further, the notion of a "gift," or "purpose," is a lofty one. It is reserved, we believe, mostly for those larger-than-life people whom you read about in newspapers but certainly do not know personally: world-renowned musicians; legendary sports stars; founders of large, successful businesses. *They were born with a gift,* you think, *not me.*

As a result of our fears and expectations, we shy away from entertaining the idea that we may actually have one: a particular, innate, overarching drive that cries out to be developed and exercised. Call it a gift, a purpose, or a passion. It is that irrepressible need we have that captures our imagination and urges us forward. It makes us, and others, smile, laugh, cry, and cheer. It is something we are compelled to do, simply because of who we are. Big or small, it makes no difference. We have little choice but to follow its call.

For some people, it is too late. Their gift has consumed them and, in the best sense, they have become its servant. Like my friend Diane, they are the truly happy ones.

> *The gift we have captures our imagination*
> *and urges us forward.*

Diane is a flight attendant. Her outgoing nature allows her to enjoy her job, which takes her around the country and around the world. As I learned soon after meeting her, Diane chose not to have children. Why she made this choice remains a mystery to me to this day, but that isn't the point. Ironically, she and her husband wound up living on a street that is loaded with kids, from infants to teenagers. And she welcomes them all.

When my friend isn't up in the air, she's digging in the earth; Diane loves gardening. In the past few years, Diane has slowly and painstakingly transformed her modest yard into a beautiful garden, filled with all kinds of plant life, both common and exotic. She has managed to cultivate raw, unassuming patches of dirt into small islands that boil over with organic art.

A year or so ago, I was visiting Diane and her husband. As I entered their backyard, I was startled by what I saw. Where there was nothing but rocks and a few plantings only weeks earlier, there was now a small pond. It had a bubbling waterfall at one end, and was filled with Japanese koi and dotted with lily pads. It had a foot-bridge that traversed its widest point, made of rough-cut flag-stones. It was stunning to see. Even more impressive than the visual transformation, Diane had built the pond with her bare hands, just as she had built the trellises that gated her garden and the pathways that defined it.

Like most of her friends, I was taken with her creation. Every time I visited, I expected to see something new. Diane's yard had become more than a garden; it had become a community. It brought people together and had evolved into a conversation piece for friends and neighbors. If you were lucky, you might visit and go home with a cutting from "Diane's Garden." It was a small victory if you did.

One day, Diane got a call from a local newspaper. They were doing a story about area gardens and had heard about hers. As she tells the story, Diane was utterly surprised. She had no idea how they'd found her and couldn't understand why they wanted to come by. A month later, I saw Diane's picture in the paper, standing resplendent on the footbridge she had crafted with her own hands.

Diane's smile is never broader than when she is guiding people through her garden, telling stories about each species, how she found it and how she brought it to life. In time, I have come to understand that what blooms in my friend's yard is more than plants. Figuratively speaking, it is her very seed. The way I look at it, my friend's instinctive, maternal need—her basic need to give— had found its natural expression.

GETTING TO THE PROMISE
OF POWER AND GRACE

The adage "It is better to give than to receive" has been part of popular culture for as long as most people can remember. But the fact is that most people spend most of their time figuring out how to do the latter. On the surface, this is understandable. We have families to feed, homes to maintain, friends to visit, presents to buy for others, and so on.

What we rarely realize is that knowing one's identity—even its formative elements—causes an unexpected thing to happen to us. We *want* to give; indeed, suddenly, we must. Why? Because we now have something of consequence to offer. The desire to give— to create something of value for people—is innate. Giving is our natural state and, once located, it will not be denied.

To live through your gift is to have found that special place where you feel most alive. It may well take the form of a garden, as in my friend Diane's case. Or it might be a factory floor, or a class- room, or a carpenter's bench. It might be an office cubicle, or a locker room. It could be an art studio, the kitchen of a famous restaurant, or the one in the back of the pizza parlor. Or the one in your home. It might be a rectory, or any one of a thousand "places" to which we are naturally drawn, where we simply love to be, and where we are loved simply for who we are.

The kind of gift I am speaking of is not to be confused with a talent, such as writing musical comedy, cooking, playing guitar or hockey, or some other finely honed, worldly skill. These talents are *expressions* of one's gift. They are not the gift itself. As I see it, Diane's garden was an expression of her gift, which might be best stated as her drive to humanize nature. Your gift is never visible. Only its physical manifestation is.

In the same vein, while you might have several impressive talents, you have only one gift of the type I am referring to. This gift flows from, and blends, the capacities that make you special and the passion that the pattern of your life reveals. Just as there is only one of you, there can be only one such gift. Your gift is the practical expression of your identity. Put in other terms, your identity is your gift to the world.

Giving is our natural state and it will not be denied.

Knowing your gift, and finding ways to give it, brings a palpable sense of peace. Your search is finally over, along with the anxiety it creates. The emptiness that has eaten at your gut subsides. Authenticity, and the strength it produces, is yours: nothing about you is made up. Nothing is fabricated to please others. In fact, finding your gift, and weaving it into your life, affirms who you are—that you are here, alive, and have a meaningful role to play in this world.

Answering the question *What is my gift?* holds out the promise of achieving both power and grace. Born of your identity, "power" isn't about controlling others. It is about taking life into your own hands; it is power for the *good*. It is constructive rather than destructive. Such power benefits all people who are part of its expression, because it is based on making a genuine and lasting contribution. Knowing your gift gives you the power to make a difference. It also bestows upon you the grace with which to make it.

When grace flows from identity it takes on special meaning. It can be seen in how you might do something inordinately difficult with apparent ease. There is grace under pressure, which gives you the strength to endure trials and resist temptation. Born of identity, grace is the state of being fully and effortlessly engaged in the world. In such a state of grace, your creativity isn't dissipated by conflict. Energy isn't wasted. Tolerance, patience, and self-assurance are your hallmarks. No one exemplified these traits more fully than Joshua Stein, a rabbi whose very presence made people feel important, even when they didn't feel that way about themselves.

Rabbi Josh, as he was known, walked with a limp and a cane. He had contracted osteomiolitis in childhood and evidence of the disease had stayed with him throughout his life. No matter; Rabbi Josh lived above his condition with ease.

Born of your identity, power is power for the good.

I have known several members of the clergy in my life, but none has had the ability to lead a congregation like he did. When he spoke, he spoke to you, despite the fact that you might be sitting at the back of the room, among several hundred people. Rabbi Josh was entirely accessible. Not just in terms of being available for private conversations, but as a person. His status as a rabbi never got in the way of his status as a human being. And that was his magic. That was the source of his extraordinary power.

Once, years after I had last seen him, we ran into each other in a restaurant in the town where he lived. Within moments, he was asking about my son and how he was doing—in school and in sports, which he loved more than anything. Rabbi Josh had never met my child, but spoke about him as though he had known him all his young life. This, too, was magical. He had an ability to sweep you off your feet with his knack for remembering the details of your life others might easily forget. He made you feel like you mattered.

> *Your identity is your gift to the world.*

Joshua Stein wore a glint in his eye that was unmistakable, below the shock of silver hair that adorned his head. He could be firm, yet he always remained mellow. His words could be critical, yet he stayed unflinchingly kind. Unlike many members of the clergy, Rabbi Josh never let his position go to his head. He remained steadfastly anchored to his heart—and to our hearts. When I think of Joshua Stein today, I think about a man who has always been more spirit than flesh, a man whose unassuming power and natural grace have brought comfort and hope to many.

FOLLOW THE SIGNS OF JOY

Most people intent on finding their gift look for clues in their work, past and present, their family backgrounds, their hobbies and interests. As sensible as this may seem, none of these factors will lead you to the answer. None gets to the heart of your remarkable capacity to create value—that distinctive contribution you are capable of making in the world.

The way to find your gift is by *following the signs of joy*—those aspects of life to which you are instinctively drawn and that stir your soul.

Joy comes before happiness. In unraveling your identity code, understanding the distinction between these two ideas is important. The definition I assigned to happiness early in the book was that you are at peace with yourself, among others in the world.

To arrive at this place, you need to make joy your guide. In the words of Joseph Campbell, philosopher and mythologist, you must follow your bliss. At its core, joy slices through the defenses, concerns, and rationalizations we use to keep ourselves balanced against the pressures of our daily lives. It leads us directly to a place of elation we have probably long forgotten exists within us. When I refer to elation, I am referring to feelings that take you over completely. For instance, that feeling of sudden heat that unexpectedly wells up in and washes over your body. Or the shudders that run up and down your spine, releasing tension in their wake.

That elation comes from an unqualified love of *something*. It can be the creative juices inside you that run free when you are cooking up a storm. It can be the feeling of unbridled awe you connect with as you gallop on horseback across open fields, deep in the heart of the mountains of Wyoming. Or, perhaps, it is the freedom you feel in your bones as your voice soars in the midst of singing a passage from your favorite opera.

> *Joy comes before happiness.*

Whatever it may be, what brings you joy carries you naturally to a state of near-ecstasy, where the tensions of the day disappear and you are one with yourself—you are at peace with who you are, among others in the world. The only thing that matters, then, is to find that "something."

Put your identity puzzle together

The beauty of a puzzle is that when the pieces come together they reveal a picture that finally makes sense to you.

Your identity is a puzzle to be solved. Once completed, it illuminates the value-creating potential your gift suggests. The main pieces of your identity puzzle include three sets of themes: the themes that define *what you love,* the theme that captures *the pattern of your life,* and those themes that define the *basic nature* of the experiences you identified at the outset, which led you to unearth what you love. By basic nature, I am referring to the innate meaning of each of these experiences to you. Combine these themes and you will have the main ingredients you need to complete your puzzle and understand your gift.

By way of example, consider Terry, whose story I told in connection with the question *Where am I going?* Three of the things Terry loved were discovery, growth, and freedom. Although I didn't present it as part of her story, the pattern of Terry's life revealed a passion for exploration, which led her to push the boundaries of her life, personally and professionally. Here is how she defined the basic nature of the activities she originally named: horses were all about *movement,* as were dance and travel; the basic nature of history revolved around the theme of *evolution;* nature was about *purity.*

Discovery, growth, freedom, and exploration. Movement, evolution, and purity. These were the central themes hidden beneath the surface of Terry's life, which, when combined, turned her identity puzzle into a picture that finally began to make sense for her. Teasing them out and connecting them to one another had enabled my friend to understand where she wanted to go and why she wanted to go there.

Your identity puzzle brings together different clues about who you are into one comprehensive picture. That picture explains how the pieces of the identity code you've discovered so far fit together. Moreover, it helps point you toward what may be in store for you, going forward.

Our identity code, much like our genetic code, is complex in its structure—it can be tricky to figure out. Our identities are the result of generations upon generations of talents, skills, and passions blended, over and over again, into distinct combinations that make us the individuals we are. While the puzzle you put together is particular to you, it also reflects the lives of people from innumerable bygone generations. In this way, it honors your past as well as your future.

Find the words

The picture you are looking for in completing your identity puzzle comes in the form of a succinct, deceptively simple statement that clarifies your gift and the value it implies. Here are three examples: *I am Larry Ackerman and I am driven by the need to help people to see; I am Terry and I am driven by the need to help organizations find the freedom to grow; I am Diane and I am driven by the need to humanize nature.*

It is literally a matter of need. That is what identity-based living is all about: following the course that pulses in you as irrepressibly as the blood that flows through your veins.

> *Your identity puzzle brings together clues about who you are into one comprehensive picture.*

In no instance does this statement—your personal identity statement—define exactly what you should do with your life. How you apply your gift is up to you. Rather, your personal identity statement reveals your potential for creating value in this world. If you heed it, it will help keep you honest in determining what path to take and which ones to avoid. It will also help you to know not only what to do but also how to do it. You may choose to stay in the line of work you're already in, but how you tackle your job may change dramatically. Or you may choose to start over and find a vocation that fits more naturally with who you are.

Draw the implications

Of all the moments you will encounter on your identity journey, the one you have now reached is filled with the greatest sense of possibility. You have arrived at the point in your journey where the prospects for realizing your potential are palpable. In deciphering your gift, you have cracked the most important aspect of your identity code—the foundation from which life is most fully lived. From this place you can move ahead, secure in knowing who you are and why you are here.

Use your personal identity statement as a lens for evaluation. Consider the possibilities your identity holds. Terry saw how changing the basic mission of the finance department would increase its importance as well as strengthen the bond she had with her boss and associates. In following this course, and making it happen, she improved her organization and honored herself.

The implications are limited only by your imagination. Organize your thoughts into categories: your work, your relationship with your spouse or partner, your relationship with your children, your church, your friends. Take your time. Let the possibilities bloom.

For the moment, it might well be enough to bask in the warmth of what you've learned. The feeling of calm you get when you discover your identity is a reward all its own and will help carry you forward with quiet confidence. You owe it to yourself, however, to bring your identity statement to life. That is how you will find integrity.

Your purpose is there, waiting for you to discover it.

The payoff in coming to terms with your gift is knowing your purpose. It is there, waiting for you to discover it. Call it your gift or your purpose; it doesn't matter. They are one and the same. Both flow from your identity and define your relationship with the world at large: from your coworkers and employer, who benefit from how you express your gift every day, to the mass of people you don't know at all, but among whom you now have a place to stand that is all your own. The sense of purpose we achieve when we know our gift fuels and enriches all of our relationships. In terms of finding peace within ourselves, knowing our gift makes us happy.

Having reached this vital point in your identity journey, you will affirm, in no uncertain terms: *I have much to give.*

EXERCISES IN REVELATION

The following exercises are the fifth part of the Identity Mapping process. They will help you *discover your gift by following the signs of joy.* These exercises are designed to respond, directly and indirectly, to the different steps presented in this chapter. In some instances, they may go beyond the examples the chapter provides.

1. **Put your identity puzzle together.** Begin by referring back to the original list of "things you love and love to do."

   · Determine the *basic nature* of each of these experiences or activities. By "basic nature" I mean the core significance of each of these experiences to you—what each activity means to you in your gut. For example, as I mentioned earlier in this section, horses fundamentally suggest *movement,* as in walking, trotting, galloping. Dance also implies *movement.* History is all about *evolution.*

   · When you have deciphered the basic nature of each activity, write it down, below the columns you originally created, with an arrow pointing from that column to it.

   · Now circle the ideas that are essentially, or literally, the same. Record below them a dominant theme, if you find one.

2. **Compose your personal identity statement.** Gather and write down all of the main themes you've identified: the themes that define *what you love,* the theme that captures *the pattern to your life,* and those themes that define the *basic nature* of the activities and experiences you named previously.

   · Now begin a sentence, "I am driven by the need to . . ."

- Look for how the themes you've written down combine with one another into a coherent thought. Feel free to shuffle, sort, and revisit these words. Even add to them if you wish (including verbs, in order to make a sentence). As another source of ideas, refer back to the lists of answers you wrote in identifying what you love. You can also put each theme, or set of themes, on a separate piece of paper and, literally, move them around.

- Complete the sentence you started above. Consider different combinations of words until one idea captures—and holds—your imagination.

3. **Draw the implications.** Once you are satisfied with your statement (you will know you are when it feels right deep in your gut), start to consider what it may mean to your life in concrete terms.

   - Organize the implications into categories: your current work and how you do it; more broadly, your career path; and your relationships with your spouse, family, and friends.

   - Carry your journal or a notepad with you and continue to jot down ideas as they come to you over the next days and weeks.

4. **Start setting priorities.** Consider how your life might change if you lived through your identity. Start small. Decide what actions you can take now that are not too challenging or disruptive. Set a calendar of events, by date and action, and follow through. Document the results your actions have had on you and others.

THE SIXTH QUESTION:

Who Can I Trust?

Individuals are inherently relational and relationships
are only as strong as the natural alignment between
the identities of the participants.

The glory of friendship is not the outstretched hand,
nor the kindly smile nor the joy of companionship;
it is the spiritual inspiration that comes to one when
they discover that someone else believes in them
and is willing to trust them.

—RALPH WALDO EMERSON

TASHA

Most people seek stability in their relationships with others. There are the "little stabilities" that mark our daily routines. They sprout from casual friendships, acquaintances, and office mates. And there are the "big stabilities" that define the contours of the time we are here on earth. These flow from spouses and partners, family members, long-term employers, mentors, and truly close friends. Taken together, the relationships we form—the big ones and the small ones—frame our lives in ways that give them the structure we need to find our way in this world.

In the absence of structure, life as we know it would be impossible. It would be random, rootless, nomadic. It is our relationships that give our lives meaning, for it is only through them that we are able to express who we are.

Achieving genuinely stable relationships is considered by many people to be a special victory. These relationships aren't to be taken for granted. Stability carries with it expectations of comfort—something you can count on, no matter what.

When viewed through the lens of your identity, however, figuring out who you can truly count on gets more complicated. Sometimes you find that stability isn't all it's cracked up to be. Or, in the case of some relationships, that it really wasn't there in the first place.

Like a prism that turns diffuse light into a spectrum of sharply defined colors, looking at life through the lens of your identity can cause you, without warning, to see your relationships in new and surprising ways. As in the case of Tasha, you become your own prism.

> *Our relationships give our lives meaning, for it is only through them that we can express who we are.*

Tasha was a poet-chemist. I dubbed her that after learning that this reserved, straight-talking research scientist wrote verse at night, after long days overseeing various experiments in the research lab of a major pharmaceutical company. I was working with that company some years ago when I met Tasha, who was one of my interviewees.

What was most striking about Tasha wasn't just the contrast between her writing verse and her writing formulas; it was that Tasha was blind. As she explained to me, chemistry, and the possibilities it held, had always been her first love in school. In time, she had found ways to make it her vocation.

Our paths had crossed coincidentally, but we shared a common bond that led us to establish a connection, which lasted several years. Our vision was the central influence on our respective lives. This bond spawned numerous phone conversations and e-mails, all of which focused on identity—hers as well as mine. Through these communications, I have, figuratively speaking, watched as Tasha has changed the physical and emotional contours of her life by examining, and in some cases dramatically altering, many of her most important relationships.

Nothing stirred Tasha more than using chemistry as a crucible for testing new compounds that held particular promise for curing heart disease. This was the area she specialized in. She spoke to me incessantly about this passion in vivid and animated terms. She talked about her need to "illuminate," or "reveal," the restorative possibilities various compounds might hold.

At times, her descriptions were even poetic. Once she said to me that a "cleaner heart would help the soul." And her numerous visual references weren't surprising at all, given her physical condition. In fact, they were constant and, as it turned out, central to understanding her gift.

Tasha was driven by one thing—the need to bring healing images to light. Not to life, but to *light*. As she explained to me, her task was to enable her colleagues to see these "images"—not just the compounds—clearly, and then take them forward to their next level of development.

Once Tasha was able to put her gift into words, I started receiving a flurry of communications from her. Each described in brief but dramatic terms the effects her now clear sense of identity was having on her relationships, in particular with her family and friends.

For most of her life, Tasha had a strained relationship with her father. He never seemed quite satisfied with her progress, despite her extraordinary achievements. He always wanted more from her. She sensed his frustration, which made her feel exposed and often uncomfortable. Still, Tasha respected her father's nagging conviction about what he saw as her untapped potential and loved him genuinely. But she was often afraid to reach out to him, for fear that he would take advantage of her vulnerability.

By contrast, Tasha's mother was overly protective. She acknowledged her daughter's success, but constantly warned her about not overextending herself. Tasha appreciated her mother's concern, which had become a refuge for her in difficult times. Yet she always wished her mother had believed in her more, rather than treating her as though she had, as Tasha put it, a "broken wing."

Within a few months after she had given voice to her identity, the way Tasha viewed and interacted with her parents began to change. She found herself actively seeking out opportunities to talk with her father. She wanted—in fact, she needed—to tell him who she really was. Her fear of his disapproval began to subside. She no longer felt vulnerable in his presence. She even began to understand that her father may have sensed aspects of her gift that she herself had failed to recognize. Tasha's identity had become the unexpected platform for spawning better communication and, in time, a better and more honest relationship with her demanding father.

By contrast, becoming aware of her identity had almost the opposite effect on Tasha's relationship with her mother. Tasha's discovery served to confirm what she always, if unconsciously, knew: that she was a whole person despite her handicap—that she had no broken wing. At first, Tasha withdrew from her mother. She needed some distance from her self-appointed "protector." As much as she loved her, Tasha now understood more than ever why she had always felt that her mother should have believed in her more.

> *She was a whole person. Despite her handicap,*
> *she had no "broken wing."*

The impact of knowing her gift had an effect on all of Tasha's relationships. Tom was one of Tasha's oldest friends. She had known him since high school. To Tasha, one of Tom's most attractive traits had always been his nonmaterialistic values. He was never particularly attracted to fancy cars, fancy clothes, or fancy watches. Trained as a lawyer, Tom had developed an active interest in how the law could help meet social challenges as well as business needs. Money was important to Tom, but it was not the focus of his life.

Several years out of law school, Tom joined a small computer company as its in-house counsel. When the company was sold to a larger concern, he made a lot of money. In the months and years that followed, Tasha watched as Tom changed. His disinterest in material things gave way to a passion for them. More than one fancy car now occupied his garage. He wore custom-made clothes. He moved his family into a much larger house.

Most distressing to Tasha was that Tom's new wealth seemed to desensitize him to social issues he had always supported: in particular, interests in environmental protection and ensuring civil liberties for people of all means.

Despite these changes, and the frequent discomfort it produced in her gut, Tasha tried to remain friends with Tom. She worked hard to speak his language and show interest in the things he was attracted to.

Becoming conscious of her identity, however, changed everything. Tasha now keenly felt the differences that marked her relationship with her longtime friend. Despite her misgivings, she began to separate herself from Tom. There were fewer phone calls, fewer dinners, fewer e-mails.

As Tasha explained to me, she had no choice. She could no longer play along with Tom in hopes of maintaining their friendship. The effort had become almost one-way, and that wasn't going to work. Tasha could no longer trust Tom as she had for decades and she knew it.

Her choice to let go of this longstanding relationship was painful, but necessary. Despite her disappointment, Tasha had followed the only course of action she could, the only one that would allow her to maintain her integrity.

GETTING TO THE PROMISE OF SANCTUARY

Trust is everywhere. Although we may not realize it, we ask ourselves the question *Who can I trust?* many times, in numerous ways, every day. Who can I trust to tell me the truth about how I look in my favorite outfit? Which painting contractor can I trust to make my house look beautiful? Who can I trust to babysit my children when I have to work late? Which past employer can I trust to give me a good job reference? Which customers can I trust to pay me on time? Which doctor can I trust to take care of my dying spouse?

The question of trust permeates our lives, touching everything from the mundane to the serious, from simple matters to matters of life and death.

When it comes to building an identity-based life, *trust* is a word that contains a mountain of magic. At bottom, trusting others—being able to rely on them to accept you for who you are—leads to peace of mind, which can be hard to find in these fast-paced, change-laden times. Where does this "magic" come from? What are its secret ingredients? You know them all: equal parts intuition, vulnerability, and acceptance.

To trust someone, you need first to rely upon your instincts about the other person's intentions. Do you sense he or she will be open to listening to you? Do you feel that the individual might also be looking for a relationship that is more than skin-deep? If the answer is yes, take the next step.

Let your guard down and take the risk of exposing your doubts and imperfections. If not all at once, then a little at a time. You need to make what amounts to the *first move:* inviting someone into your world without knowing in advance whether he or she will accept or reject your invitation. Finally, if a meaningful two-way dialogue does ensue, you must accept the real possibility that what you think, feel, and do may actually change as a result of the trust you've place in this person.

> *Let your guard down. Take the risk of exposing your*
> *doubts and imperfections.*

Trust doesn't happen just to grown-ups. I recall how Ruth, the fifteen-year-old daughter of a friend of mine, was struggling in school. She would pour herself into soccer, which she loved, and her social life, which, not surprisingly, was fast becoming an all-consuming experience. School came last, and Ruth's grades for the past three years reflected it. It wasn't a matter of intelligence; Ruth was above average in terms of her IQ. It was simply a matter, as she put it, of "wanting a life." Translated, that meant wanting to enjoy herself. School was work, and that didn't fit her worldview.

No one could get Ruth, now a high school sophomore, to see the value of studying, until she met Ben. Ben had been assigned to partner with her in her biology lab. For some reason, the two became fast friends. Ben was a good student—not exceptional, but solid. Ben became Ruth's confidant. She was outspoken with Ben concerning her feelings about school. She also told him about her dreams of playing professional sports—dreams, she allowed, that her family just wouldn't understand. She trusted that Ben wouldn't judge her, but would simply listen, which is what he did.

According to her father, Ruth came home after soccer practice one day and disappeared into her room. All she wanted was to be left alone. Late in the evening, she emerged with two quizzes she had recently taken, one in history and one in biology. She handed them to her parents. The former was graded a B-, the latter a B+.

Her father, surprised and delighted, asked her what had happened. "Nothing," she replied. "I just decided it was okay to make school a part of my life. Ben wants a life, too, and school works for him, so I guess it can work for me."

Finding people you can trust is both easier and harder once you have a clear sense of your identity—once you know your gift. It is easier in that your identity automatically acts as a filter, enabling you to weed out people whom you may like, and even admire, but who you know aren't really in tune with who you are.

> *Finding people you can trust is both easier and harder once you know your identity.*

I recall how keenly my friend Diane was able to discern whether someone she had met perhaps only once or twice was likely to turn out to be a good friend or remain a pleasant acquaintance. She'd spend time with them in her garden, showing them around and sharing stories about what she termed "nurturing nature." In short order, Diane was almost always able to conclude one of two things. On one hand, she might say to herself, *This person appreciates who I am, she understands my need to give through the beauty of my garden—I can trust her.* Or my friend might say, *This person acknowledges the pleasure I take in gardening, but doesn't recognize its meaning to me—I like him, but can't really trust him.*

It is also harder to find people to trust once you understand who you are. It is harder for two reasons. First, knowing your identity makes you infinitely more discriminating about what matters to you in life. The stakes are higher. Your integrity hangs in the balance of nearly every decision you make. You simply know better what contributes to your happiness and what is merely expedient.

Second, the field of candidates narrows dramatically. *Trust* is no longer a term you automatically assign to everyone you call a friend, or even family. In fact, *trust* is no longer even a word; it is a blessing you confer upon people who, by their actions, honor who you are. They alone deserve it.

Answering the question *Who can I trust?* brings with it the promise of sanctuary—special relationships that become places of refuge, that protect and nurture the most sacred and beautiful aspect of your being. Within these sanctuaries, you can recharge your engine with people who know what matters to you and who want what you have to give.

> *Knowing your identity makes you infinitely more discriminating about what matters in life.*

TAKE STOCK OF
WHO MATTERS AND WHY

There are many ways to describe the sanctuary identity-based relationships provide. Consider these relationships resting stops you can count on to be there when you need to take a break. Call them filling stations for your soul, manned by individuals who can offer needed criticism as well as support, but whose criticisms you welcome because they are stoked by a deep regard for who you are and what you love.

The sanctuaries I am talking about are safe havens where you can share fears about your own limitations, as well as dreams about how life might be were you to overcome them. They are even places where sparks can fly and creation can occur spontaneously, resulting from the electricity generated by aligning your identity with someone else's. Such creation can take many forms: for instance, the seeds of a new business venture, the idea for a movie, a theme for a local arts festival or an inventive cookbook—even a child.

Amid all the relationships you have today and will form tomorrow, only a few will qualify in terms of providing you the sanctuary identity-based trust brings. The way you will know if they do is by *taking stock of who matters and why.*

Define your relationships universe

To know who you can trust, begin by defining the universe of relationships that frames your life. Consider these relationships the "stars" that populate your universe and inventory them all. Your relationships universe naturally includes your family, friends, work associates, and others who are integral to your life. Take other people into account as well; people who don't necessarily fit into one of the obvious categories, but to whom you are instinctively drawn.

One might be your longstanding hair stylist, who has heard as much about you over the years as your closest friend has. Another might be your gardener, with whom you share a beer or a glass of wine now and then, once the lawn has been mowed or the bushes trimmed. Alternatively, you may find yourself thinking repeatedly about your minister, or rabbi, or even the quiet, unassuming assistant to the minister, whose character you've always admired but with whom you have never spent any time. If you are a student, such people can include a favorite teacher or guidance counselor.

The process of developing my relationships universe led me into unexpected corners of my life. I found myself recalling friends I had made in elementary school whom I hadn't seen for years. Now men and women, these were childhood peers who had penetrated my psyche in positive ways and who, to this day, remain important in my life. There was Bill, today a construction project engineer, whose house was my second home through junior high school. There was also Steve, who, as a fellow Boy Scout, helped me learn how to tie knots, pitch a tent, and sneak out of it at night without being caught.

The more varied your relationships universe, the richer the results will be as you begin to take stock of who matters and why. You will then be in the best position possible to identify which stars are likely to shine the brightest and which, in time, may gradually fade.

Create your inner identity circle

Among all the stars in our solar system, it is the sun we count on to supply the energy we need. In the same way you need the sun to live, you also need a small group of relationships—one carved out of your relationships universe—that becomes your "inner identity circle." The people who come to occupy this circle are those who genuinely want the fruits of your gift and who are willing to give to you in return.

Your inner identity circle will become a true source of energy, in good times and bad times. Over the course of your life, you may expand, or narrow, your circle. Whether your identity circle contains three people or six isn't important. What is important is that everyone within it honors your identity as well as their own.

Taking stock of who matters and why isn't a black-and-white exercise. Deciding who fits within your circle doesn't mean that someone—a friend, parent, sibling, teammate, or business associate—is automatically in or out of your life, depending on whether they've "made the cut."

Neither does "fit" depend on being geographically close to someone else, or on seeing that person regularly. I often think about Richard, whom I haven't seen in years. I met him in college. Richard and I became close friends and spent much of our time together until our respective vocations led us to opposite coasts.

We were very close. At first, Richard and I would simply share a bottle of cheap wine, usually at midnight as we devoured a pizza, sitting on the floor of the dorm room we both inhabited. In short order, we started sharing secrets and concerns, as well as our hopes, aspirations, and frustrations. About school. About girlfriends. About careers, which, at the time, were little more than abstractions.

We discovered common ground in our shared passion for human achievement. For instance, Richard pushed himself hard and cajoled others to do the same. Then, as now, I have always believed in the power of human potential and have worked to help realize it, when I can.

Despite the distance between us today, Richard retains a spot in my inner identity circle and will forever. The bond your identity creates with others defies time and transcends place.

Trust exists on many levels. There are people you can trust to be honest and faithful and true to their word. But that doesn't mean they belong in your inner identity circle. Identity-based trust is a world all its own. It grows out of a shared view about what is fundamentally right and true. It springs from passions and priorities both of you hold dear. It is fueled by the unspoken, often unconscious, knowledge that the other person could, if necessary, represent your opinion to others flawlessly—and that you would trust him or her to do so, without hesitation.

> *The bond your identity creates with people defies time and transcends place.*

The deep-seated intimacy identity-based relationships spawn doesn't mean that there isn't room for disagreement. In fact, it is precisely because your identity and the other person's identity are in sync that you can argue vigorously, or debate fiercely, without fear of rejection. Traditionally divisive topics such as politics and religion are no match for the therapeutic undercurrents that flow from your identity.

Building relationships with individuals whose identities align with yours makes caring for all people easier. When you know who you are, you become more accepting of others. You no longer gauge your own worth by how others perceive you, or how you perceive them. You have found sanctuary in your relationship with yourself. As a result, you can be compassionate, even loving, toward people without necessarily bringing them into your identity circle.

Trust yourself first

Finding sanctuary in your relationship with yourself isn't always easy. It is often easier to listen to other people's heartfelt opinions and adopt them as your own, especially people whom you instinctively want to trust. This may be your partner, your mother or father, your boss, or your lifelong best friend.

Even when you feel a knot form in the pit of your stomach, you still may lean toward the words others speak. Sometimes they will be right, at other times they won't. But that isn't the point. The simple expression "Trust your gut" is filled with wisdom, especially when it comes to matters of identity.

> *When you know who you are, you become more accepting of others.*

You have come a long way on your identity journey. You have decoded many aspects of yourself that you may not have even been aware of until now. Trust what you have learned. The answers to what is right or wrong for you are readily available, waiting for you to uncover them, without assistance from others. Trusting yourself is loving yourself. It is the necessary first step in learning to love, and be loved, by others. I know this firsthand.

Strapped down on the operating table in the hospital when I was a toddler, in the midst of my living nightmare, all I wanted was for my father to come and rescue me. Even though I was unable to move, I imagined that I was reaching out for him, looking over my right shoulder to the doors I had just passed through, where my father and I had parted company.

Slowly I realized he wasn't coming. I was all alone. In that moment, I concluded that the reason he wasn't there was that I had done something terribly wrong—exactly what, I didn't know. Still, I reasoned, it was my fault I was on that table. In the moments that followed, as my throat tightened and I lost my ability to breathe, I also lost faith in myself. I no longer trusted myself. Somehow, I reasoned, I had let my father down and was no longer worthy of his love.

It has taken me years to unravel the tangled threads of this experience, to make sense of it, and, finally, to learn to trust—and love—myself once again. There is no middle ground when it comes to trusting or believing in yourself. Either you do or you don't. In truth, however, you have no choice but to do so. That is what the Law of Relationship demands.

If your inner identity circle is to have the power to be self-sustaining, you need to be its first member. Some people will come into your circle and some will leave. That is to be expected over the course of time. But yours is an irrevocable lifetime membership.

Give and take

You can't trust someone who doesn't trust you in return, no matter how much you may want to. If you extend your hand in an effort to establish, or deepen, a bond and the other person doesn't reciprocate, you automatically clam up. You protect yourself, instinctively. This is an involuntary, perfectly normal reaction: *you know better.* You know that what is most exquisite in you can be given only if the other person is prepared to give as well.

Consider the seesaw. Many of us grew up on playgrounds and in parks, where seesaws were a natural part of the surroundings. One person would mount one end of the seesaw, while someone else would sit at the other end. The idea was to move up and down in unison. As one person pushed off, the other person yielded to the momentary power of his or her companion.

Done properly, both children experienced the thrill of the ride. But if one person jumped off, the seesaw ceased to move and it ceased to be fun. In fact, it could be downright uncomfortable, if you were the one left sitting on the board with your knees hunched up around your shoulders. Give-and-take creates a sense of flow between two people. It is a simple philosophy that applies to building trust just as it does to playing on a seesaw.

When I first understood and articulated my identity I felt a great sense of peace and relief. I also began to ask myself some new and challenging questions: To whom would I give the gift my identity revealed? Who would benefit from it the most? Who would actually want to see through clearer eyes? Who would want to see the opportunities hidden under layers of unexamined assumptions about how life works, or the vital connection between their past and their future? Who would care? Who could I count on to value what I had to give and who would respond in kind?

Trust creates an *us* that requires both people to open up simultaneously. In many ways, the kind of trust that flows from identity is an act of validation. It exposes, connects, and, in turn, validates the most deeply human traits in one person with those in another.

To know who you can trust, ask yourself whether each of the people who compose your relationships universe cares about the things you love. Do they respect what is most important to you? Can you speak freely with them about who you are? Listen to your answers honestly.

To take this step, you must first be honest with yourself. You must answer these questions: Have I told others about myself? Have I talked with them about what I love? Have I described to them what my gift is? Have I reached out first to establish trust? That is your responsibility. You are in charge.

> *Trust creates an* us *that requires both people to open up simultaneously.*

As important as it is to give, it is equally important to take, since trust is a two-way street. Based upon your relationships with different people, determine who you believe will be equally open with you about themselves. Then test the waters. At meetings, dinner parties, outings, quiet conversations, ask people questions like these: What really matters to you in life? If you could be remembered for one thing, what would it be? If you could change the world, what would you change and how would you do it? Who are you without your job, your money, your family?

If, after a few tries, the answers you get seem cold, or if you don't get any answers at all—only blank stares—you will know you have reached the limits of that relationship. Perhaps you can trust that person on simple matters, but not on matters that would lead you to expose your identity, and its meaning, to them.

If the response you get from someone is pensive, listen to what he has to say. Encourage him. Lead him. Let him know that it is safe to open up, that you will respect his vulnerability. Be patient.

> *Who are you without your job, your money, your family?*

If the person you are addressing appears relieved that you brought her to this level of communication, embrace the moment. Let her speak. Share stories. You have found a true star in your relationships universe. Perhaps one worthy of joining your inner identity circle.

Expand your horizons

Just as astronomers strive to discover new stars as they explore the universe, it is important for you to keep your eyes open for opportunities to meet new people whose passions align with yours.

In many ways, your horizons will follow the contours that form your relationships universe. They will be most evident in how you organize your day: through your work, friends, church, sports, or any other arena that defines the structure of your life. Search each of these venues. Let each become fertile ground for finding new people who will benefit from your gift and who, in turn, you will honor by accepting theirs.

Some years ago, a woman I know, Lauren, participated in a two-day, thirty-mile walkathon in New York City, organized to raise money to fight cancer. Her sister was suffering from the disease and she decided that this event would enable her to do something to honor her sibling while helping to combat the disease.

The experience led her to cover a healthy portion of the city, along with hundreds of other people. In the "tent city," where many of the participants stayed overnight, Lauren wound up sleeping next to a woman named Jen, a cancer survivor who was only twenty-three years old.

Lauren and Jen spent a good part of that night trading stories about their lives, despite having been exhausted by the day's trek. With little prodding from Lauren, Jen related her story—not just about her experience with cancer, but about her past: her upbringing on the South Side of Chicago, the untimely death of her mother, her admiration for her brothers, who were in the military. Jen's matter-of-fact openness and her obvious courage were infectious.

Lauren talked about growing up in a small town in Pennsylvania and her solo forays to Europe during college, where she had to fend for herself, with no family around. She spoke most of all about her love for her sister, who, she confessed, had been more like a mother to her than their mother had been. She was terrified of losing her sister—a thought that haunted her more than she cared to admit.

In the crucible formed by that special night, Lauren and Jen connected in ways that defied the short time they spent together. The next day, they completed the walk arm in arm as they crossed the finish line. Lauren and Jen have stayed in touch ever since. As

Lauren frequently reminds me, the depth and meaning of her conversations with Jen go well beyond even those she has with people she has known all her life.

Being open to opportunities to expand your horizons will keep you alert and in close touch with yourself. Sizing people up through the lens of your identity will help you learn who you can trust, instinctively. It will also help you cultivate your identity, causing it to take root, ever more deeply, into your being. Expanding your horizons will become a lens through which you will routinely take stock of the world and ultimately find your place in it.

Living by the Law of Relationship holds out the prospect of sculpting a life that testifies to the power you hold—the power to positively influence not just your own path but the paths of those people whose lives you touch through your gift.

When your relationships are fueled by this power, you are fully engaged in life. You are operating under "full sail." This is the reward of taking stock of who matters and why. And it is in having reached this place that you will avow: *I need others and am most productive with those who need me in return.*

EXERCISES IN ASSESSMENT

The following exercises are the sixth part of the Identity Mapping process. They will help you *know who you can trust by taking stock of who matters and why.* These exercises are designed to respond, directly and indirectly, to the different steps presented in this chapter. In some instances, they may go beyond the examples the chapter provides.

1. **Create a list of "influentials" in your personal identity journal**—family members, friends, work associates, and others who are integral to your life—people whose influence is great and/or whose opinion you value highly.

   Once you have exhausted these sources, expand your list to include people from different areas of your life, such as your church, sports teams, volunteer organizations, even alumni from your college or high school. Also, consider the people who "tend" to your life, such as gardeners, hair stylists, barbers, and others, whose influence may be modest, but whose work you admire and company you enjoy.

2. **Identify people with whom you have had intimate conversations in the past.** By "intimate" I mean *below-the-line* conversations, where you talked about life issues. Conversations in which you were able to express doubts, hopes, and fears, and the other person was able to reciprocate.

3. **Evaluate who you feel will want what you have to give.** Based on your relationship with each person you've named, beginning with those in exercise 2 above, ask yourself these questions:

   • Does he or she care about the things I love?

· Does he or she respect what is most important to me?

· Can I speak openly with him or her about who I am?

You need to be prepared to tell people about yourself if you haven't already: for instance, what you love, what your gift is, and why it matters. If you've kept this information to yourself, it will be harder to make the correct evaluation at the outset.

4. **From the list you've created, determine who you believe will be equally open with you about themselves.** You can gauge this, initially, by trusting your instincts about the people you've identified. Either you know them well already, or you sense there may be some bond between you.

   · First, simply imagine a conversation with each of these people, where the topic has something to do with identity. As though it were a scene from a play, pay attention to the dialogue, specifically to the responses you imagine them giving you. Make note of these responses in your journal.

   · Next, ask challenging questions. In settings where you feel comfortable, pose questions that will make people stop and think. They can take many forms. Here are three for you to consider:
     If you could be remembered for one thing, what would that be?
     If you could change the world, how would you do it?
     Who are you without your job, your money, your family?

5. **Cross-reference your answers to questions 2 and 3.** Write down the names of the people who best meet the criteria for both questions. For each person, decide what actions—they can be large or small—you feel are necessary to get the most from that relationship in the future. Pick one action for each

person and carry it out within a month. Regardless of the outcome, record it in your journal. Continue to make entries describing how that relationship evolves over time.

6. **Prepare to make changes.** Based on the results of what you have learned and your actions so far, let the process work. Allow some relationships to deepen and gradually let go of others.

7. **Keep your eyes open for new opportunities.** Identify new people who may prove to be kindred spirits. Make mental notes of new acquaintances at work, in school, at parties, or in church or community groups whom you want to get to know better over time. Write down their names and the reasons you are initially attracted to them as potential identity partners. Get to know them. Trust yourself.

THE SEVENTH QUESTION:

What Is My Message?

THE LAW OF COMPREHENSION

A person's various capacities are only as valuable
as the perceived value of the whole of that person.

*I had found a kind of serenity, a new maturity . . . I didn't
feel better or stronger than anyone else, but it seemed no longer
important whether everyone loved me or not—
more important now was for me to love them.*

—BEVERLY SILLS

CHLOE

One of the things people try to discern when they're attempting to figure out who you are is what you stand for. They want to know what cause, purpose, or passion fuels the choices you make in life. Sometimes they poke around silently, in the course of conversation with you, searching for clues. That person wants to know, but, making little progress, may conclude that there is no answer to such a seemingly cosmic question. Or he or she will pursue an answer through others who know you well and are regarded as reliable sources.

In trying to figure out what you stand for, what people ultimately want to know is whether they can relate to you, and, if so, how. No matter what the outcome may be—a deep and abiding friendship or a superficial nod—they are looking for a frame of reference they can count on.

Telling people what you stand for explains and exposes you in your entirety. Not trait by trait, skill by skill, or talent by talent, but you, as a complete and undivided being. That is its power and also its danger.

Letting others know what you stand for takes courage. Telling your story can be a risky proposition. You risk rejection, as when someone concludes, after hearing your story, that they respect you but don't necessarily want to spend time with you. You risk losing support in the form of votes if you're running for public office and voters don't like what they hear. You risk loss in a variety of other forms as well: for instance, loss of a job if you let your boss know that you can't go along with a course of action you fundamentally disagree with; or loss of a lover who, once discovering what you truly stand for, is suddenly less attracted to you than he or she was just the day before.

> *Telling people what you stand for explains*
> *and exposes you in your entirety.*

What you gain in telling your story, however, is worth the risk. For every relationship that may end, a new, more genuine one is likely to begin. Having endured the discomfort that change invariably brings, you gain self-esteem. You gain confidence. You gain the ability to sleep at night, every night. No one I know demonstrates this reality better than Chloe, a friend who has experienced the liberating power of telling people what she stands for.

I met Chloe at a conference in Chicago a decade ago, where I was speaking about the impact of identity on career choices. During the break after I was done, I noticed her snapping pictures of attendees as she made her way through the crowd, and I asked her what she was looking for. That is how we crossed paths.

Chloe lived in a well-to-do Chicago community where she, her media-executive husband, and their two sons enjoyed a very comfortable lifestyle. Although Chloe was at the conference to explore possible vocational paths for herself, she spent most of our few minutes together telling me about the joys and challenges of raising her young children, including her recent stint as president of her local parent-teacher organization. It was clear to me at that moment that Chloe's sense of identity revolved firmly around being *Mommy,* despite her obvious interest in expanding her personal horizons.

Beneath her warm and charming exterior, I sensed Chloe's struggle. On one hand, she was the socially correct mother-wife, a community leader, and a friend to many, with obvious skills in all of these areas. On the other hand, she had come to this career conference intent on figuring out who she was as, simply, herself. It was that struggle that captured my imagination and made Chloe interesting to me as a person. It was that struggle that made Chloe human.

About a year after we met, Chloe and her family moved to Connecticut. Since then, we have become good friends. I have come to see the person behind the mother-wife, and to hear the story of who Chloe really is.

Raised in an upstate New York town, Chloe had a remarkably simple upbringing compared to the one she now enjoyed. Not wealthy, not privileged. Down-to-earth and straightforward is how she described it.

If there was one thing Chloe's unassuming past had teased out of her it was her passion for truth. This passion wasn't some philosophical pursuit; it was visceral. Chloe felt most comfortable amid things that were authentic and unadorned. "True things" is how she put it.

This passion had influenced many aspects of Chloe's life. Eventually, her passion for truth influenced how she performed in various jobs. In one case, Chloe's job was to buy network television time for a consumer products company. In her role, she met often with important clients and was asked by her boss to wear certain kinds of clothes that he felt would reflect her professional responsibilities. These were ultrasophisticated fashions, which made her feel decidedly self-conscious. In her words, Chloe felt like an "impostor." The dress code just wasn't who she was and it grated on her. Despite her business success, my friend left that job after only a few months.

About two years ago, our families were having dinner together at Chloe's home. I noticed a stack of photographs in a corner of the kitchen, which I began to thumb through. There were pictures of her kids and some mutual friends. There were shots of a sunset taken at the local beach. There were images of a group of dogs playing together and of children I didn't know. All of them were in black and white.

When I asked who had taken them, Chloe acknowledged that she had. Her answer to my question, however, was filled with unspoken questions of its own, which I discerned beneath her words: Did I like what I saw? Did I feel it was strange that she was showing an interest in photography? What did I think of her in this new, unfamiliar context?

I was genuinely impressed with her efforts. They weren't run-of-the-mill pictures; they showed thoughtful composition. They were spontaneous. They had an undercurrent of joy.

When I inquired why her work was in black and white, she told me that color only got in the way. Of what? I asked. "Of the truth," she responded. "Color," she continued, "was irrelevant." To her way of thinking, black-and-white images were timeless creations. And that is exactly what she sought through the lens of her camera.

In the many times we have gotten together since then, I have watched as Chloe has continued to wield her camera in the name of "timeless creations." One day, in the local newspaper, I noticed a picture of a sports event—a volleyball game at the beach at sunset—that was hers. There, below the picture, was her name in small print. In my mind, that photo credit amounted to a few formative "words" in the message my friend was finally beginning to send.

Chloe's growing interest in photography slowly began to bear fruit in the form of family essays and landscapes, for which she was paid by friends and, occasionally, local publications. One afternoon, I happened to praise Chloe on her mounting achievements. Instead of smiling and simply accepting my words at face value, she looked at me with doubt in her eyes. There was tension in her voice as she responded to my compliment.

Chloe spoke to me as though she had been rehearsing her words, not for moments or even hours, but for months, perhaps even for years. My casual demeanor gave way to intense concentration.

In an almost apologetic voice, Chloe explained that ever since high school she had been fascinated by photography. It allowed her to be invisible. It was like being in hiding, yet always in a position to capture what was going on around her. Being in that "hiding place," yet connected to her surroundings through her camera, made her feel alive.

Over the years, her pictures had become the most important gifts she gave to people. What made them special, she stressed, was the fact that her works were always a surprise to the individual who received them. She would never allow herself to be seen taking pictures of her subjects. And she would never show people samples of her photography during the event, or occasion, she was attending. She would wait until the event was over before sending her pictures. Knowing that her subject wasn't expecting the photos thrilled Chloe. It underscored the fact that her pictures were truly gifts, in the best sense of the word.

> *Color only got in the way of the truths her photographs revealed.*

As she spoke, Chloe's eyes brightened noticeably. "My heart," she said, "races when I hit the *send* button on my computer. I know then that I have committed myself, through my work, to others. I am sending, I guess, the truth."

She paused. Then Chloe looked away from me as she continued. Her words caught me off guard. In measured tones, Chloe confessed that she had always felt that someone had to be rich and a bit weird to be a photographer. Rich because cameras were just so expensive, and weird because the photographers she had known, or read about, seemed offbeat and eccentric—not like "normal" people.

But Chloe was neither rich nor weird. Despite her love of the art, she could never be these things. This belief had haunted her for years. As a result, she would never use the word *photographer* in relation to herself; she didn't want to be an impostor.

Several months later, I went to a photo exhibit where Chloe was showing some of her work. As I entered the crowded hall, I noticed that my friend had placed a large stack of business cards on a table near the door. I had never seen them before. It jarred my senses.

There she was, for all to see: my friend, the *photographer.* There must have been a hundred cards in that stack, if not more. Along with her name, phone number, and e-mail address, each card contained two small but striking black-and-white pictures of former portrait subjects. These two tiny pictures set her cards apart from all the others on the table, which were purely text.

I spent about an hour at the exhibit looking at Chloe's work and the work of other local photographers as well. I watched as Chloe chatted with people about her images and, I imagine, about their photographic interests and needs.

As I was leaving, I glanced at the table in the front of the hall and noticed that Chloe's stack of business cards was now a fraction of its original size. Exactly nineteen cards remained. I smiled. Chloe had finally figured out her message and had sent it—in the form of two-inch by three-and-a-half-inch business cards—for all to see. She had faced her fear of rejection as an "impostor" and survived. And if I read her message correctly, the truth I believe she loved the most was her own.

> *She had faced her fear of rejection as an "impostor" and survived.*

GETTING TO THE
PROMISE OF LIBERATION

What is my message? is a question that has an outsized impact on our lives, even when we aren't aware of it. We are forced to answer the question frequently, and in all sorts of ways. It comes up in the essays we write as part of our college applications, where admissions officers strain to figure out which candidates to accept and which to reject. The question raises its head again as we search for jobs after graduation—whether from high school, college, or graduate school—and are faced with the not-so-simple task of expressing who we are on one or two pieces of paper called a résumé.

If you are fortunate and succeed in your job, you come face-to-face with the question again as you rise through the ranks to a supervisory, or leadership, position. What is your message, then, to the people who work for you? Not what tasks you want them to do but, rather, why they should follow you, beyond the fact that you're their boss.

The question slips into our lives on more modest levels as well: for instance, at large social gatherings and community get-togethers, when you are introduced to people for the first time. Or at intimate dinner parties, when you are one of only a handful of people who are thrust together for three or four hours and need to figure out how to keep the conversation going.

In all of these situations, you have choices to make. You can try to discern what is important to others and tell them what you believe they want to hear. You can supply information you feel is safe and easy for others to relate to (in Chloe's case, that she was a past PTO president and mother of two boys, rather than someone whose passion for photography belied her love of truth). Or you can make a point of finding ways to tell people something about who you are at your core, and risk making yourself vulnerable, if only for the moment.

The fact is that taking the "safe" route isn't safe at all. Most people, from college admissions directors and would-be friends to the people you work with and who report to you at work, are searching for clues about you that make you human. They are searching for signs that give them reason to believe you are someone they should take a chance on, and possibly trust.

There is more. Hiding what you stand for takes a toll on everyone. It may make it easier for you to navigate business or social relationships that require chameleonlike skills to maintain, but over time it erodes your sense of self-worth: you know you're faking it. Moreover, keeping your true self hidden makes life harder for others by keeping them guessing—off balance, in fact.

People who want to know you better need you to let them in. For all the time you may spend with them, over months or even years, friends, bosses, mentors, even partners and family members, can't read your mind. They can't peer inside you to see what makes you tick, what you love, what gives you joy. Yet they may sense there is more to know about you than you've let on to them so far. So they stand there, figuratively speaking, with one foot off the ground, waiting patiently to find out. When it comes to sending your message, what seems safe isn't. Time is running out.

There's a well-worn expression that the whole is greater than the sum of its parts. It refers to the notion that the pieces of something—for instance, a cathedral made out of hundreds of thousands of bricks, or a company composed of many divisions—add up to something greater than the pieces themselves.

> *Hiding what you stand for erodes your sense of self-worth.*

Despite its widespread use in business circles and other areas of life, we rarely recognize that the most dramatic example of this idea is each of us, the individual. Our "parts"—the arms, legs, heart, brain, skin, eyes, and so on—are nothing compared to the result that comes from their miraculous integration into the unique human beings we are. That is how we assess people: as complete beings. And nothing makes you more complete than your identity. Put in other terms, your message is found in the wholeness of your being, not in your parts. It is a message the world needs to hear.

It wasn't until I faced an auditorium full of people, prepared to affirm my passion for identity, that I finally felt ready to let the world know what I stood for. For years, I lived under the radar. While assisting companies and individuals I knew who I was, and, certainly, I let my passion for identity show in everything I did. Yet I never had the courage to stand up and be counted in a public setting. I had let my writings and my work speak for me. Now I would speak for myself; I would make my message clear: *I am Larry Ackerman and I am driven by the need to help people to see.* As I spoke these words, I exhaled deeply. I felt completely naked as I stood before my audience, knowing there was no going back. I was finally free.

Answering the question *What is my message?* holds out the promise of liberation—liberation from the fear of being who you are and doing what you know you must. Liberation brings with it the self-confidence to not be deterred by what others may think of you, no matter who they are. Yes, you may face the prospect of rejection by people who matter to you. And facing that prospect will take courage. You may also realize that you no longer have a choice: *you must take a stand.*

> *Our "parts"—arms, legs, heart, brain, skin—are nothing compared to the miraculous integration that results in the unique human beings we are.*

Often in the course of our lives we arrive at a point where we run out of excuses: why *not* to do something, why *not* to follow a certain path, why *not* to take a particular risk. For all of the excuses we've come up with over time, we haven't gained the recognition we've been waiting for, or the money we sought, or the love we wanted. At that point, we are finally ready to tell the world what's really on our minds. We are ready for liberation.

DECLARE YOURSELF ON
THE STRENGTH OF YOUR GIFT

Liberation isn't so much a physical state of being as it is a feeling that rumbles deep in your bones, seeking to be found. There are many ways to describe the feeling I am talking about. They all start with captivity.

In the course of our lives, we turn ourselves over, time and again, to people and organizations in order to be accepted, paid, loved, nurtured, or recognized. It is what we do to get along. We are all born with values and convictions we cherish, with identities that are the essence of our being. But over many years, we put these powerful forces on hold, because that is what we must do to belong—to companies, to clubs, even to families. Sometimes we are conscious of the choices we make. At other times we make these choices unwittingly. Either way, we allow ourselves to be imprisoned.

After a time, the weight of captivity becomes too much. This happens as your identity blossoms, as it expands to the point where it can no longer fit inside the cage that contains it. When you reach this point on your identity journey, emancipation is all that matters. What you seek is deliverance.

The promise of liberation is all-consuming. The feelings that shake your bones reach a level of intensity where they simply must be released. They demand to be heard. How, then, do you realize the promise of liberation? By *declaring yourself on the strength of your gift.*

Declarations are serious business. They imply a commitment to follow one path and walk away from others. Declarations are about choices that aren't easy to alter, such as the major you must declare in college, which reveals something about your interests, tells the world where you plan to focus your studies, and, possibly, even what line of work you may pursue.

What makes declarations so powerful is their intent, which, in short, is to *remove doubt*. It is to make something clear in people's minds that wasn't clear before. Declarations lift the veil of mystery. They state something emphatically, often for the first time. When Chloe placed that stack of business cards on the table at the photo exhibit, she was removing any doubt as to what her gift was: to give people truth through pictures. Now her conversations with others would be more open, more focused, more meaningful.

Knowing your gift is the key to declaring what your "major" should be in life. It is the living, practical expression of your identity. It is the content of your message.

For all its magnificent power, many people hesitate to send their message. Not because they don't know what it is, or even because they're afraid others may not like it. The real answer is surprising. Secretly, what many people fear is the power they will gain when they finally do send their message, because it means that they are truly on their own.

Sometimes, without realizing it, we let ourselves come to depend on others to take care of us, long after we've reached adulthood. They—a parent, friend, boss, or well-meaning mentor—tell us who they think we are, or should be. Consciously or not, we follow their lead. It is comfortable, even reassuring, to be under someone else's wing. But once you declare yourself, you officially detach yourself from your caretaker. You are wholly responsible for what happens to you in life. You are now the master of your own fate. You are the captain of your own ship.

Working to decipher your identity code puts you on a path that leads, inevitably, to a moment of unguarded declaration. In that moment, the seemingly rational logic that led you to hold back from taking a stand in the past gives way to the logic of the soul, which urges you forward. Reason recedes as you present yourself to the world, not to be judged but to be seen in the light your identity casts. In that moment, the outcome in terms of what other people may think of you doesn't matter at all.

> *Knowing your gift is the key to declaring what your "major" should be in life.*

Rehearse your message

Even the most accomplished musicians rehearse their music before they go onstage. The artist may have sung her song a hundred times before, but the act of rehearsing refreshes her memory, reawakening the music inside her, as though she were performing it for the first time.

Before sending your message, rehearse the experience in your mind as well as in reality. Imagine a dialogue with people you trust deeply. Imagine that they are inquiring about your purpose and your place in the world, if not in so many words, then by virtue of the subject at hand. Topics revolving around career paths, who your friends are, or choices regarding what school you're planning to attend ultimately are informed by your identity. With people whom you don't know well, requests such as "Tell me about yourself" and "Tell me about your past" are clear invitations for you to describe who you are.

Some years ago, I attended a conference on leadership. The keynote speaker, a bright, passionate young woman, asked audience members, who were seated at round tables, to introduce themselves to the person sitting next to them. The charge was to tell your neighbor something about yourself that went beyond the usual job description, something that revealed a bit about who you were as a person.

What sticks in my mind to this day is the story of one particular man. He was the chief financial officer of a large and well-known Dutch company. His title and credentials, along with his dark suit and starched white shirt, were imposing. His story, however, revealed more about him than his attire and position did.

He explained that he was born and raised on a small farm in the backcountry of the Netherlands. As a young boy, he rode tractors with his father, which he recalled easily and spoke of with affection. He learned what hard work was from an early age. His schooling was modest. He wound up going to college fairly close to home, since he didn't have the grades to get into a university in England, which is where he had wanted to go. It had taken him a while to realize he was pretty good with numbers, but after he did, he began to seek out jobs where he could apply this natural skill.

Finally, with a soft chuckle, he admitted that it was hard even for him to believe that he had wound up working for such a large international concern: "The farmer's boy turned financial executive," as he put it. Almost as an afterthought, he added that he had learned about the importance of numbers early in life, when, every day, it was his job to count the number of eggs his family's hens had laid, so they could be properly accounted for before being packaged for sale.

I thanked him for sharing his story, and as I did I saw this man in a new light. In a matter of a few, short moments, the Dutch finance chief in the dark suit had become human before my eyes.

Whether you know them intimately or have only recently met them, practice telling people about yourself. Weave into your conversations bits of information about your sense of purpose and its relevance to them and to life, generally. Learn to tie your gift to the topic at hand.

Rehearsing your message will help you understand the many implications your gift holds with respect to the choices you will make throughout your life. You will be in a position to consider different possibilities as you prepare to take the stage.

Find your forum and tell your story

As you rehearse your message in your mind, you are likely to find yourself returning to one particular "place" over and over. Perhaps you imagine yourself in a college classroom, or at the podium at an important conference. Possibly, you keep coming back to a meeting room with dozens of people in your church hall, or at your office with a handful of trusted associates.

> *Practice telling people about yourself.*
> *Tie your gift to the topic at hand.*

What you are looking for is a comfort zone in the truest sense of the term. Your task is to seek out, or create, real-life settings where you will have an opportunity to talk about needs and opportunities that call upon you to let people know what you stand for.

I have found many forums in which to tell my story over the course of my life. The first was in the shelter of my rabbi's office. He was a man I had known since I was in my teens and I had come to trust him deeply. From there, I moved to telling my story, if only parts of it, to the participants in reading groups, where we were supposed to relate what we were reading to who we were.

My forums became more public as my self-confidence grew. After a few years in consulting, I graduated to telling bits of my story in front of clients who I sensed would be open to hearing the truth about identity and how it affected their organizations as well as themselves. In short order, my forums came to include a few speeches and conferences. But it was several years before I would find the courage to tell my story—to truly declare myself—in an auditorium, in front of hundreds of people whom I had never even met.

In time, you will be able to deliver your message almost anywhere. With practice, it will become second nature. The value of comfort, at this moment, is that it allows you to focus, without distractions, on the challenge at hand. You will know you have identified the right place when your natural instinct is to relax when you arrive.

The prospect of delivering your message to others—of declaring yourself—can be as frightening as finding yourself in the middle of a dense forest on a moonless night. You're not sure where to turn, but you know you need to keep moving. Finding the right forum to tell your story is like coming upon a welcoming campfire in the midst of the forest: the territory may be unfamiliar, but for the moment you are calmed by the fire's warmth. You are at ease.

> *In time, you will be able to deliver your message almost anywhere.*

Live your words

It is accepted wisdom that actions speak louder than words. It is our nature to look for concrete evidence that someone means what they say. Chloe's business cards were hard evidence of her commitment to be, and be seen as, a photographer. For all their seeming modesty, those cards were an invitation to people to engage Chloe on new terms—not just as the socially accomplished mother-wife, but as an individual who created value in her own, special fashion.

Your message isn't a message until you send it. It can be "sent" in many ways. It can be sent verbally, in the form of a speech to a crowd, or through a simple conversation with a few people. You can deliver your message in how you spend your time and the priorities you live by.

A message isn't a sentence on the notepad that sits on your desk or bedside table. Nor is it a discussion you would like to have with your parents, teacher, boss, mate, or best friend. A message connects you with others directly. A message is all about action.

The act of declaring yourself brings with it the obligation to live your words. What you are likely to find, in fact, is that when you're ready to send your message, you are more than ready to live it. You will be hungry to perform.

Following a recent speech, I left the stage exhausted and exhilarated. I spent the next twenty minutes fielding questions during the break. I was anxious to touch as many people as I could in the short time I had before I needed to leave. One conversation still resonates in my mind.

A middle-aged manager from an aerospace company was grilling me on how to get his senior executives to consider adopting identity-management practices as a way to develop better leaders. Five minutes into our conversation, the man stopped cold. He looked at me and told me that my talk had meant a great deal to him personally. He was, he allowed, an alcoholic and the question of identity burned inside him.

In that instant, our relationship went from pleasant to profound. We spent nearly an hour in a nearby meeting room, where I listened to him intently. I felt a deep sense of responsibility and the urge to help him. After a few minutes, I explained how he could begin to address his issue constructively and walked him through a few simple exercises. Most important, I assured him that an answer to his question was there to be had.

> *When you show the world who you are, you become your own force of nature.*

You can travel a long way down the road your identity reveals and still not be known for who you are. That is a distressingly restless place to be. For, after all the work you've done to decode your identity, you are left feeling incomplete. Perhaps feeling good inside about what you've accomplished, but still lacking the profound sense of satisfaction that comes from getting through the experience of taking a stand, making yourself vulnerable, and letting others line up behind you, or not.

When you show the world who you are, you become your own force of nature. You become a center of gravity that will inevitably attract some people, repel others, and, as a result, orient the world you choose to inhabit.

When you finally tell the world what you stand for, you will declare what you've known all along: *to establish meaningful relationships, I must first be recognized for who I am.*

EXERCISES IN DECLARATION

The following exercises are the seventh part of the Identity Mapping process. They will help you *figure out your message by declaring yourself on the strength of your gift.* These exercises are designed to respond, directly and indirectly, to the different steps presented in this chapter. In some instances, they may go beyond the examples the chapter provides.

1. **Imagine a dialogue with people you trust deeply.** They are inquiring about your purpose and aims in life.

   • Refer back to the people you named in your answer to question 5 at the end of the last section. What are the two most important things about yourself you want these people to know?

   • Write down why each is significant to you and how it affects, or might affect, their lives.

   • Consider you are writing a play or a movie script. Write down, in short lines of dialogue, the gist of how such a conversation might unfold, given what you know about the people you named.

2. **Find an opportunity to engage each person you named in a real conversation.**

   • Directly or indirectly, talk about your gift and how it contributes to—or could contribute to—your relationship with them.

   • Record in your journal how the actual conversation went, compared to the one you imagined.

3. **In your mind, practice telling an audience about yourself.** Imagine a public forum, large or small, in which you tell people what matters most to you and why it is, or should be, relevant to them. Consider different situations: your workplace, parties, your parents' or child's home, your church, a community or town meeting. Write that statement in one or two sentences.

4. **Identify real-life settings where you will have the chance to talk about challenges that call upon you to give your gift.** Consider family get-togethers, support-group meetings, weekends away with friends, or your workplace.

   • Choose the best setting in which to have this conversation—someplace where you feel comfortable and, generally, at ease. Make a plan to make this happen within a month.

   • Record the result of this conversation in your personal identity journal. Describe how the interaction made you feel. Was it a generally positive experience? A negative or uncomfortable experience? Provide details that illustrate your reaction.

   • Describe what, if anything, you would do differently next time and explain why.

   • Decide when your next best opportunity may be to declare yourself and make plans to take advantage of it.

THE EIGHTH QUESTION:

Will My Life Be Rich?

THE LAW OF THE CYCLE

Identity governs value, which produces wealth,
which fuels identity.

———

*Until one is committed, there is always hesitancy, the chance
to draw back. Concerning all acts of initiative and creation,
there is one elementary truth, the ignorance of which kills
countless ideas and splendid plans—that the moment
one definitely commits oneself, providence moves too.*

—W. H. MURRAY

DAVID

For many people, dreams about how their lives might turn out are the stuff of dinner party conversations: tasty fantasies, fragrant desires, and pungent images that spice up otherwise dull table talk in revealing ways. When dinner is over and your guests leave, they take their dreams with them until the next time you meet, when those dreams once again boil up.

This pattern can continue for a lifetime, until you've given, or attended, your last dinner party. Then your dreams, like leftovers left too long in the refrigerator, turn stale. They become worthless.

For some people, these conversations are enough. They are warmed by the possibilities they describe, and at the same time comforted by the distance between themselves and the meal they imagine. Despite recurring pangs of hunger, they are as full as they dare to be.

Other people's appetites are larger. The life they envision is redolent with hope. The pangs of hunger they feel are impossible to ignore. Figuratively speaking, the kitchen becomes their home. They set about preparing to do whatever it will take to turn their dreams into reality. Like my friend David, they have chosen to turn their special recipe into a lifetime of sustenance.

I met David just after his divorce, and as he was looking for a new job. David's life had already taken several turns. He had graduated from a prestigious business school two decades before we met. Subsequently, he had worked in his family's thriving construction business, started his own venture capital concern, and followed that with an industrial design company. All of David's efforts had been reasonably successful, financially speaking. Yet none of these jobs was enough to satisfy my friend.

David is a big man: six feet eight inches, about 275 pounds. In physical terms, he gives the decided impression that he can pretty much do whatever he sets his mind to. I sensed that David was a man on a journey, not physically speaking, but spiritually. At the age of forty-five, however, it wasn't clear to me where his journey was taking him.

He and his new wife, Joanne, whom he married shortly after we met, lived in a lovely Colonial-style home not far from my home. It was filled with antiques: not the rare and expensive kind, but the kind that come from modest, overstocked stores you find in the New England countryside. The kind that exude simplicity.

If David had one steady passion, it was his church. He spent hours volunteering for projects that stole time on weekends and sometimes even intruded on his work. As I soon discovered, this passion of his wasn't just about being a good citizen and helping out.

As time passed, David talked more and more about his love for his religion—David is Episcopalian—and how it shaped his view of life. He started working with the rector of his church. He helped out regularly at Communion. He began talking with his minister about subjects for sermons he felt were timely and important.

David brought his love of religion to the many dinners we shared together. Not in a preachy sort of way, but in a way that invited discussion. He talked about how Christians and Jews shared the same God. He pointed out other similarities, rather than the differences, between the faiths.

When he spoke, David radiated warmth, excitement, and serenity all at once. I vividly recall a moment when David and I were on a fishing trip together in northern Maine. During a lull in the action, we were talking about the nature of God when suddenly it occurred to both of us that there was no greater evidence of His "nature" than the beauty that surrounded us as we sat in our boat. David looked at me, smiled, and said, "See what I mean? Nature doesn't belong to one religion or another."

> *David radiated warmth, excitement,*
> *and serenity all at once.*

David had an extraordinary talent for making religion a comfortable subject for all people to talk about, no matter what their particular faith might be. His generous view of life enabled him to wrap his long, large arms around everyone in amazingly non-threatening ways.

David's journey had picked up speed. One year later he told me of his decision, which he had been hinting at for quite some time: he was going to quit the business world and join the seminary. He and Joanne were going to sell their home and most of their possessions and move into a small apartment in New York City on the grounds of the seminary he was to attend. He would sell his interest in his industrial design concern to his partner and wrap up any other outstanding business affairs. He had made his choice and Joanne was supportive. David was going to be a minister.

I was not surprised; I was in awe. I was witnessing one of my best friends not only declare himself but give himself over entirely to his passion—to the true work of his life.

Two months later, I spent a Saturday helping David and Joanne pack up their possessions. We sorted out what was to be kept and stored, what was to be sold at a tag sale, what was to be given to family members, and what few things they would take with them to the tiny apartment that awaited them. I felt as though I were in a movie, taking part in someone else's life-changing drama. In essence, that is exactly what I was doing: helping my friend methodically disassemble, one piece at a time, the many things that had marked his life to date. David's dream was fast becoming his reality.

Today, David is a minister for a Connecticut church, preaching on Sunday mornings, comforting parishioners when needed, spreading his particular brand of faith among people fortunate enough to be a part of his flock. We still see each other often. We break bread and drink wine together. We talk about everything, from fishing to God.

When I look into my friend's eyes today, I see joy. Not that his life is easy, or even simple; it isn't. As David admits, being a minister is demanding work. Still, as I listen to him describe his days, it is hard for me to know whether David is giving more than he gets from people or getting more than he gives them. On balance, it really doesn't matter. My friend pursued his dream and has become a wealthy man.

GETTING TO THE
PROMISE OF ENDURANCE

Asking ourselves whether our lives will be rich is one of those questions that make us sweat. Some people sweat from the anxiety that comes from simply not knowing the answer. Others sweat from the burning hope that maybe someday they will make it big, cash in, hit the jackpot. Any reference to *rich* instantly conjures up images of money and the things money can buy. These things can range from luxury cars and fancy homes to fine educations for our children and, perhaps most of all, the supposed freedom from worry that "being rich" implies.

Still others sweat because they realize that if they stick to the course they're on, the answer to the question *Will my life be rich?* will probably be no. Their sense of responsibility to their families, their well-meaning efforts to protect what they've accumulated, or to acquire more of it, have taken over their lives. Along with their jobs, their days are governed by "to-do" lists, mortgages, tuition payments, soccer games, lawn mowing, bake sales, dance recitals, church suppers, and on and on. Despite the satisfaction many of these experiences may bring, they have squeezed out any hope of giving voice to the deeper passions that keep these people alive inside.

People are sweating the wrong things. For all the time you invest in trying to "know" how things will turn out in your life, what actually happens to you in the future remains a mystery. For all the effort you may put into getting rich in financial terms, unforeseen circumstances can derail your dream. For all the energy you invest in owning up to the fact that you've left no room in your life for you, regret will accomplish nothing.

What *is* worth sweating is whether, from this day forward, you do right by yourself and by others. This sequence—first you, and then other people—is deliberate. It is only when you build relationships that reflect who you are at your core that you can "do right" by other people. Your identity is the *living lens* through which you can safely engage the world, make informed decisions, and thereby fashion a life that you, and others, can trust.

> *What* is *worth sweating is whether you do right by yourself and by others.*

It is also worth sweating how you define *rich*. There is nothing wrong with money. There is no nobility in your being poor, any more than there is in your being financially well-off. As much as wealth may be about money, however, it is equally about those things that, like a magnet, draw people back to you over and over again. For instance, the heartfelt recognition you receive from friends and family members that fuels your determination to redouble your efforts at whatever you did to win that recognition in the first place.

The idea of attaining a "rich life" is an invitation for you to decide what truly matters. What are the things that, when combined, will add up to a life you will be proud to call your own?

Finally, it is worth sweating what your legacy will be. Will the commitments you make and the actions you take today leave people better off because you were here? Will Diane's green thumb nurture green thumbs in others over time? Will the market-research organization George established become a platform where the next generation of curious minds can develop its skills at this challenging profession? Will Chloe's children as well as her clients look back at her life many years from now and thank her, yet again, for the special gifts she gave them?

The question *Will my life be rich?* isn't just about today; it is equally about tomorrow. It is about how you will be remembered and what you will be remembered for.

Doing right by yourself, deciding what being wealthy means to you, and imagining how you want to be remembered are definitely worth sweating over. For the answer to the question *Will my life be rich?* brings with it the promise of endurance.

I'm not talking about what it takes to run a ten-mile road race, cross a raging river, or swim the circumference of a windy lake. I'm talking about what it takes to endure as a human being in the face of rejection, when your friend of ten years decides you're no longer as easy to get along with as you were before you began your identity journey. Or in the face of loss, when your boss concludes that your newfound courage to speak your mind no longer fits with his idea of what makes a good employee, and she fires you. Or in moments of self-doubt, at two o'clock in the morning, when the path you've chosen to take isn't entirely clear in terms of where it's leading you.

> *What are the things that will add up to a life you will be proud to call your own?*

I'm also talking about another kind of endurance, the kind that allows you to endure in the face of time and, inevitably, in death. The Law of the Cycle is the story of infinity. Perhaps as human beings we aren't in a position to endure in the physical sense of living forever. But in the spiritual sense we are. What you leave as your legacy will produce value long after you are gone if you give your gift, no matter what it is, no matter how large or small it may be.

Where does endurance come from? The kind of endurance I'm talking about comes from having a sense of wholeness about yourself. That grounded sensation you get when you feel complete as a person: no disconnected or missing parts, psychologically speaking. Endurance comes from being in sound shape emotionally. From being able to survive intended as well as unintended blows to your ego and the anger, hurt, and disappointment that inevitably follow. Endurance comes from simply being honest about who you are, and who you are not. It comes from being deeply comfortable in your own skin. In short, endurance comes from having integrity.

> *What you leave as your legacy will produce value long after you are gone.*

SURRENDER TO THE PULL OF IDENTITY

The way to realize the promise of endurance is by *surrendering to the pull of identity*. The notion of surrendering to anything may sound bleak at first, as though you are giving in, giving up, throwing in the towel, admitting defeat.

For some people, the idea of surrender can conjure up unsettling images. You might imagine you're being asked to leap off the edge of a cliff, with no ground in sight. Or to jump into the deep end of a pool, where there is no visible bottom. These are scary thoughts. Not surprisingly, they may lead you quickly to ask yourself whether you're crazy even to consider surrendering.

You're not. Surrendering to the pull of your identity is like tumbling into the safety net that has always been there for you, waiting for you to see it and take the plunge into its woven warmth. What you are doing is handing over the reins of your life to the part of you you can count on the most to make wise decisions, to build meaningful relationships, to guide you through pain, to steer you to a place in this world you can call your own. Surrendering to the pull of identity is what it takes to do right by yourself and, in turn, by others.

Let your identity guide your days

We all face responsibilities, which shape what we do every day. Household chores, business meetings, schoolwork, addressing the needs of fickle customers, carpooling, and a thousand other obligations call us to do their bidding during our waking hours. The idea that we can simply walk away from these responsibilities and follow a different path may be attractive, it may even sound romantic, but it is hardly realistic. Neither is it realistic to throw up your hands and conclude that your present situation leaves no room for shaping an identity-based life.

Many of your responsibilities are opportunities to let your identity find expression. In meetings with nervous customers, think how you might describe what makes you the right person for the job, based not on your technical skills or years of experience, say, as a carpenter, but on what you love to do in life and how that shapes the homes you build, or the bookshelves you craft.

In the midst of a car full of chatty ten-year-olds, ask each one of them to chat about what makes him or her special as a person and how those traits relate to what they want to be when they grow up. Their particular answers aren't important. What matters is that you've given them the chance to experience what identity tastes like, if only for a moment.

If you are a student, consider how your gift influences what you want to say in the essays you write.

> *Hand over the reins of your life to the part of you you can count on the most.*

A few years ago, I hired a young woman named Sarah as a consultant. She had spent the prior three years with another firm, where she performed well, but felt constrained by its highly quantitative approach to problem solving. She had been well trained for her job, having received a graduate degree in business from a prestigious university. But something was missing for Sarah; she needed more.

What intrigued me most about Sarah was her personal background. She was a classically trained violinist and avid art lover. She spoke fluent German and passable French. Sarah had traveled extensively across Europe and Latin America. In short, there was a lot going on inside Sarah; this young woman was about a lot more than "the numbers."

As we worked together on various projects, Sarah seemed to blossom like a flower that had been left inside a windowless room for too long. The notion of identity was easy for her to grasp, both personally and professionally. She once said to me, "Finally someone is interested in who I am and how that affects what I can do." Yes, I assured her, I was.

In the two and a half years we spent together, Sarah let her natural love of music flow into her work. She wrote in simple, elegant prose, freely interpreting complicated issues with insight and ease. More than once, Sarah told me how happy she was to have joined our firm, how she felt free to bring the best of herself to bear and to not have to rely only on the "hard facts" to make the case to our clients.

Month after month, I observed how Sarah's innate creativity awakened as we puzzled through identity assignments together. My greatest pleasure, however, wasn't in the conclusions we would draw or even in the actions our clients took as a result of those conclusions; it was in having reconnected Sarah with herself in constructive ways. In return, the quality of her work took care of itself.

When you let your identity filter into your daily routine, you give it voice, allowing it to color the very things you may unconsciously wish you could simply escape, at least for a time. A surprising thing will happen to you when you follow this course: you will start to relax. Mundane tasks that weighed you down yesterday are imbued with new meaning today. They become more than just acceptable; they become important vehicles for giving your gift, if only in modest and fleeting ways.

As you transform daily acts into acts of identity, the seemingly unbridgeable divide between who you are and what you do will begin to close. You will have found the pathway for bringing the best of who you are to unsuspecting souls who will benefit from your outstretched hand.

Honor yourself always

Life is peppered with seductions waiting at every turn to lead us off track. There are small seductions, such as the unexpected invitation to play a round of golf Saturday morning rather than fix the fence around your yard, which you've been meaning to do for weeks.

> *Let your identity filter into your*
> *daily routine. Give it voice.*

There are larger seductions, too. For instance, allowing yourself to take a job you really don't want because your best friend just joined the company and she told you how terrific it is. Or going to the movies with your buddies when you should be studying for your biology final the next day. Seductions are all around us.

My friend Tasha, the poet-chemist, finally decided to let her relationship with Tom, her lifelong friend, slip away. She simply couldn't continue to pretend to like what he liked, or want what he wanted: the money, the larger house, the accolades from those who had "made it" in the business world—accomplishments that for her were just not that important.

Creating a rich life for yourself is a matter of discipline. Avoiding seductions is part of the process. Do not let yourself be seduced by career opportunities that are simply glamorous, or higher paying, but demand that you leave your identity at home. Follow your instincts. Avoid what is expedient, or merely socially correct. Be honest with yourself at all times.

As you go forward, begin to make choices that call upon you to give your gift. Choices about your career or vocation, about assignments to volunteer for in your present job, and about which ones to avoid. About the kind of people who you sense will make good friends—those you feel you can trust—versus those who will never become more than passing acquaintances.

Remember that your gift isn't tied to a particular line of work, or job. It is always ripe for reinterpretation. It is ageless. What does this mean? It means that your value in this world doesn't end if you decide to retire. Make living your identity your career and "retirement" will become irrelevant. You will be in a position to renew yourself always.

> *Do not let yourself be seduced by career opportunities that demand that you leave your identity at home.*

There is a man I once read about who was the superintendent of schools for a small town outside of Detroit—Dr. James Waters. Dr. Waters had spent most of his career moving up the administrative ladder: from head of the guidance department at a relatively young age to assistant principal to principal and, finally, to superintendent. His career spanned forty years, during which time he hired, fired, and got to know virtually everyone connected with that school system. Dr. Waters was well liked and successful. His unbridled love for, and belief in, education was well-known. Under his direction, the school system grew in physical terms as well as in the eyes of the state. Student enrollment tripled. Academically speaking, his was a top-ranked district.

> *Your gift isn't tied to a particular line of work, or job.*
> *It is always ripe for reinterpretation.*

Dr. Waters retired at the age of sixty-eight. Rather than disappear into retirement, the former superintendent became a coach. He traded his administrative role, where he had little direct contact with students, for one where he became personally involved with young people in need of expert counseling on how to navigate the choppy waters of high school, including how to balance academic pressures with social pressures, as well as the pressures that come with playing varsity sports.

From overseeing a few thousand students, Dr. Waters became a student advocate, one student at a time. Now he had a chance to take what he had seen, done, and learned over four decades and apply it, one-on-one.

Not long ago, I had the good fortune to meet Dr. Waters. He appeared as the article had described him: slightly built with a ready smile and bright blue eyes. He seemed utterly young for his seven decades of life on this earth. I saw in him a man reborn, rekindled by his passion for education, now channeled in a new and exciting way.

In the course of our brief conversation, I asked him why he decided to launch his new career. He looked straight into my eyes and told me that he had always wanted more personal contact with young people, but didn't have the chance, owing to his administrative responsibilities. Now he did. That, it turned out, wasn't the whole story. A moment later, he let his guard down and told me the following tale.

Dr. Waters had served in World War II. At the tender age of nineteen, he was thrust into the Battle of the Bulge, one of the signal conflicts of the war. All around him he saw mass confusion, along with death and destruction. Despite his duties as a soldier, he felt lost and increasingly unsure of himself. He needed help. In the months James Waters served amid the horrors of that place, someone—he never mentioned who—"bailed him out," as he described it, when he needed it the most. He had found someone he could talk to, someone who kept him emotionally sane.

That experience had stayed with him his whole life. Now he had the chance to help kids who needed some extra guidance getting through the "battles" high school inevitably presents. "Payback" was how he described it to me. He felt he had a debt he needed to repay, and educational counseling was his currency of choice.

Dr. Waters paused when he was done recounting his story. Then he concluded with this thought: if you don't reach out beyond yourself to others, you never really grow up. That he was doing, in spades.

You have traveled a great distance on your identity journey. You have survived doubt and rejection. You have overcome fear. You have discovered striking truths about yourself that have been waiting for years to be unearthed and embraced. You have what it takes to live a rich life. Use your identity as a lens through which to engage the world. Honor what you have worked so hard to find.

Make sure you are paid

Identity-based living isn't an act of altruism, where you give with no expectations of getting something back. The identity-based life

169

demands wealth in return for value. No self-denial. No misguided sacrifice.

Identity-based living demands mutual respect. The fact that you are willing to stand up and be counted for who you are is an act of bravery that demands acknowledgment from others. In this regard, the identity code is a code of honor.

> *You have traveled a great distance on your identity journey. You have what it takes to live a rich life.*

A good friend of mine, Paul, always dreamed of running a general store akin to the kind that were common fixtures on the streets of American cities and towns perhaps a century ago—small, inviting shops teeming with fresh vegetables, quality canned goods, meats, fresh fish, and a range of beverages, including soda and beer. Aside from certain modern touches, it was to be a replica of a store from a bygone era, with every manner of staple on its crowded shelves. For Paul, this store wasn't simply a business venture.

Previously, Paul had been a high school history teacher with a particular passion for learning how people were able to get along before telephones and computers took over our lives. No one could tell stories about "the old days" better than my friend, even though he was born long after the era he studied had passed.

At first, Paul's venture thrived. It attracted plenty of traffic: people who loaded up on merchandise and those who simply cruised through the aisles out of curiosity. Everyone who passed through the store was delighted to soak up the atmosphere Paul had painstakingly re-created. At first, my friend went so far as to set his prices low enough to mimic even that facet of the era he was attempting to replicate. It was all part of his dream, part of how he intended to give his gift.

Within a few short months, it became clear that his prices—a big hit with his customers, not surprisingly—weren't going to be enough to sustain his business, even though he had organized his venture very carefully. As he slowly increased his prices, store traffic began to wane. Paul's Pantry, as the store was known among his loyal supporters, was losing ground to grocery chains and other modern-day operations.

One evening, Paul confessed to me that he could most likely find a way to keep prices low, keep his store open, and eke out a small profit if he made some adjustments. These would include narrowing his range of goods, modernizing the lighting, and getting rid of costly antique fixtures, among other concessions. Paul wasn't smiling as he spoke.

It wasn't the financial realities that weighed on him; the problem for Paul came down to a matter of integrity. As my friend explained, starting his own business was never the main goal. He wasn't compelled to be an entrepreneur just for the sake of being his own boss. Paul's goal was to bring a bit of the past to life in ways he could share with others, while celebrating what he loved so much. It had now become clear to him that too many compromises would have to be made. And that when he was done making them, what he'd be left with would not express the vision his passion had inspired.

Reluctantly, my friend decided to close his store. Paul's Pantry would, ironically, become a part of history itself. As Paul explained to me, it wasn't worth keeping the doors open if he couldn't keep his dream alive. Today, his integrity intact, Paul has returned to teaching high school history. He teaches with renewed vigor, with the spirit of a man who has the courage to be true to himself.

When looked at through the lens of identity, the notion of compensation takes on different layers of meaning. For you to attempt to make a profit without first making a meaningful contribution is a recipe for failure, whether that "profit" is money, reputation, or some other form of currency. It is equally a recipe for failure for you to give your gift and not be rewarded for it in return. You deserve credit for your efforts in ways that are significant to you. You've earned it.

An identity-based life needs to be fed. Being rewarded for giving your gift is the sustenance you will need in order to endure. That sustenance can take many forms that go beyond money. These include love, admiration, thanks, reputation, or even simply a heightened sense of self-esteem that allows you to sleep better at night. No matter what you seek as your reward, make sure you are paid.

As you gradually surrender to the pull of identity, you will see how life is ordered by the intimate relationship the Law of the Cycle reveals: that *identity* (the confluence of your unique characteristics) governs *value* (the particular contribution you are capable of making in this world), which, in turn, produces *wealth* (the harvest you will reap as a result of what you give). Embrace this reality and your life will be richer. Embrace the fact that identity organizes life.

> *Being rewarded for giving your gift is the sustenance you will need in order to endure.*

The continuous cycle, from identity to value to wealth and back to identity, gives new meaning to the term *life cycle*. Look upon your identity as both a beginning and an end. It is the source of your uniqueness and potential. Your identity is equally the beneficiary of its own strength. Exercise and express it and it will grow ever deeper and more powerful in its impact on your life and the lives of others.

Endurance, in its many forms, is the reward that comes from surrendering to the pull of identity. It is in having the courage to follow this path that you will realize and assert: *I will receive in accordance with what I give.*

The following exercises are the eighth part of the Identity Mapping process. They will help you *determine whether your life will be rich, by surrendering to the pull of identity.* These exercises are designed to respond, directly and indirectly, to the different steps presented in this chapter. In some instances, they may go beyond the examples the chapter provides.

1. **Clarify what *rich* means to you.** Consider every aspect of your life today, in terms of the relationships that frame it. These are the building blocks of your future.

   - Write down the "ideal state" for each of these relationships—how you envision they would work were you to bring your identity to bear on them.

   - Specify what would be different and what would stay the same.

   Your relationship with your work:

   > **Your job**
   > **Your career**

   Your relationships with your family:

   > **Specifically:**
   > *Your mother*
   > *Your father*
   > *Your sibling(s)*
   > *Your children*

   Your relationship with your partner or spouse:

Your relationships with friends:

Specific (by name)

Your relationship with others, spiritually and in terms of important activities:

Your church or synagogue
Your interests and hobbies

2. Paint a narrative picture in your journal of how you would like your life to be in the future, if you lived according to who you truly are.

- Write a short, descriptive essay—at least one full page— taking into account the people, work, and activities most meaningful to you. Date the entry.

- Come back to it once every six months. See how close you've come to fulfilling your description. Note what you have achieved in the word picture you painted. Identify what your next steps are to continue to move forward.

- Edit and add to your picture freely as you surrender to the pull of your identity.

A Framework for Living

Most people seek order in their lives. It helps them avoid the confusion, the chaos—even, at times, the feelings of madness—that can otherwise creep up on them when they least expect it. Order helps us navigate uncertainty, deal with surprise, and explain why various events happened, or why they didn't.

Order is a matter of rhythm. Whether in the form of an utterly simple tune or a majestic symphony, music needs a clearly defined rhythm in order to be played by musicians and understood by listeners. Our lives are no different. We are our own music. We must find our own rhythm.

Look around and you will see any number of ways people find the rhythms that help them make sense of the world. Some people turn to religion to define what is right and what is wrong, what is good and what is evil, what is dangerous and what is safe, what is true and what is false.

Other people live by science. They are rationalists at heart. If something can't be validated empirically, then it doesn't exist. For them, life begins and ends with touch, sight, hearing, smell, and taste—the five senses we use to map the physical world. Still others reach for the stars. They swear by the power of the moon and the movement of the planets. Astrology is their universe. Horoscopes are the verses of their bible.

Identity-based living has a rhythm all its own. Rather than coming from some mysterious force outside of us, however, it comes from within. The rhythm of identity flows from the uniqueness and potential that defines every human being. It comes from you.

At the end of each section, I reveal the particular insight you will gain from having answered the question at hand. Embrace the Law of Being, for instance, and you will know what it means to "be alive." Accept the Law of Individuality and you will comprehend the fact that you are, indeed, "unique." Let the Law of Constancy lead you to unveil the pattern of your life and you will come to see that you are "immutable, even as you grow and evolve."

Each of these insights yields a vital part of your identity code. But there is more contained in the Laws of Identity than you have experienced so far. There is more for you to know about how these Laws bring order to your life.

> *We are our own music. We must find our own rhythm.*

THE ARC OF IDENTITY

Since the beginning of recorded time, we have organized our lives around it. We have awakened and gone to sleep by it. People have built economies to its unshakable cadence. We have worshipped in response to its steady flow. Rising in the east and setting in the west, the arc of the sun has governed our lives forever.

When the sun "goes down," as it does every evening, we don't take its disappearance as some sort of permanent loss. We know that the sun will be with us again in a few hours, to illuminate a new day. We bank on this timeless reality. Consciously or not, we are reassured by the arc of the sun and all it means to our very ability to survive.

In similar fashion, the Laws of Identity form an arc that is equally predictable, reassuring and recurring in how it frames our lives. This arc, the *Arc of Identity,* has five distinct stages, which illustrate how an identity-centered life unfolds. These stages are Preparation, Discovery, Trial, Transformation, and Integration.

Stage 1, *Preparation,* comes from having defined yourself as separate from all others. You've allowed yourself to find your "separate space" within the many relationships that frame your life. You have geared yourself to see with greater clarity than ever before. You have prepared yourself to begin your identity journey. You are *ready.*

Stage 2, *Discovery,* stems from having unearthed what you love and finding the pattern of your life. You have done the spadework necessary to find capacities and passions, which, most likely, were invisible to you at first. You have learned that your life isn't simply a series of random experiences. Rather, it tells a story that explains past events and foreshadows your future. You are *learning.*

> *The Arc of Identity has five distinct stages: Preparation, Discovery, Trial, Transformation, and Integration.*

Stage 3, *Trial,* comes from having encountered—and survived—the inevitable frustration and doubt you experience once you've gained insights into your unique strengths, but before you know exactly how to apply them. Despite all you have learned about yourself so far, you aren't yet sure where you are going. You are *tested.*

In stage 4, *Transformation,* you enter your most profound period of development. You have followed the signs of joy and discovered your gift. You have taken stock of who matters and why, and come to know who you can trust most deeply. You have declared yourself on the strength of your gift and made your message clear. In this stage, you will have taken many vital steps to align how you live with the purpose your identity reveals. You are *growing.*

Stage 5, *Integration,* flows from having surrendered to the pull of your identity. Yielding to its power, you are forging a life rich in the things that matter most to you. You have come to terms with who you are and have experienced the unmistakable sense of completeness that establishes your integrity. You are at peace with yourself and alive with purpose. You are *whole.*

THE ARC OF IDENTITY

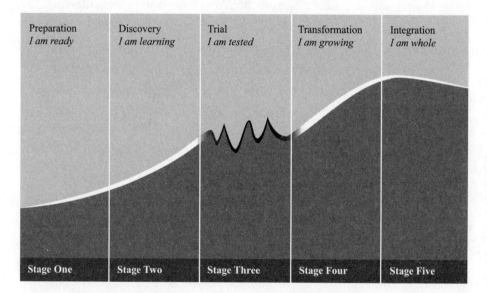

| Preparation | Discovery | Trial | Transformation | Integration |
| *I am ready* | *I am learning* | *I am tested* | *I am growing* | *I am whole* |

Stage One | Stage Two | Stage Three | Stage Four | Stage Five

Naturally, this simple description of the Arc of Identity belies a far more complex reality. The value of this description, however, is that it reveals the remarkable changes you will experience as you follow its course.

The Arc of Identity suggests that your journey will occur in discrete stages, one after another. But the journey isn't a linear path. You will revisit different stages at different times, circling back to one or more of these stages as you learn more about yourself. As you do, you will move ahead with greater conviction than ever before, on the strength of what you've learned. The process is fluid. It will respond to your touch.

I remember vividly the moment I was able to put my identity into words. I lived off the power of that experience for months. Technically speaking, I had entered my transformation stage and was growing as a result of my breakthrough.

Suddenly, I felt like I had stalled. It was as though I had hit a wall on my journey. As I look back now, I realize that despite my great gains I needed to regroup. Before I could figure out who I could trust, let alone declare myself in a public way, I needed to "get ready" all over again. I needed time to find the courage to accept the possibility of rejection that my actions might bring.

Your identity journey can start at any time. If you are wise beyond your years, it might begin in your teens, or early twenties. If you are like most people, it will start later in life, in your thirties or forties. The substance of your journey can be completed over a few years, or it can extend over decades. Its length will depend on how much the journey means to you, on how important it is to you to find your purpose and place in the world.

In the context of the eighth question, I mentioned that the promise of living a "rich" life is the promise of endurance. Not endurance in the physical sense, as all of us will someday die, but endurance in the sense of how you live on, through your gift and the legacy you leave.

Like the irrepressible rebirth of the sun each morning, the arc of your identity can begin anew after death. It can be rekindled through your children, whom you have blessed by showing them the power and beauty of living through their identities. It can carry on by virtue of how you have influenced friends to find the courage to make their identities the gyroscopes of their lives. The arc of your identity is made to endure.

THE IDENTITY CREDO

Each of the insights the Laws of Identity reveals has a value all its own. Each takes you a step further along your identity journey, helping you find ever greater comfort and meaning in who you are.

Beyond the Arc of Identity, there is yet another way in which the Laws of Identity bring order to your world. Taken together, the eight insights form a credo. This is *The Identity Credo* and it illuminates how your life will unfold when you live according to it.

I am alive, I am unique, and I am immutable,
even as I grow and evolve.
To truly live, however, I must express myself fully,
and in this regard, have much to give.
But to do so, I need others, and am most productive with
those who need me in return.
To establish these relationships, I must first
be recognized for who I am,
and it follows, then, that I will receive in accordance with what I give.

When you decipher your identity code, you will discover many wonderful secrets—strengths you weren't aware you had, passions that have lingered patiently just out of sight, and courage that has simmered just below the surface of your skin. Surrender to these forces and your identity will become the framework for living that it was intended to be. You will find the kind of happiness I described early in this book, where you are at peace with yourself. You understand your unique capacities, and live according to them. You are *happy* being who you are, among others in the world. Consider your identity your source of life. It makes you vibrant, wise, agile, powerful, even playful. It is the sun within you, whose energy need never die.

Take the Identity Credo as an invitation to make your journey one worth remembering. Cut your own trail through the forest we all inhabit and encourage others to do the same. Challenge people to raise the stakes, where letting down your guard and expressing who you are define the nature of your relationships with them.

There is no easy path when it comes to unleashing the remarkable energy your identity contains. There are no shortcuts. But you already knew that. Let your commitment to an identity-based life inspire others. Be their guide. On the strength of your success, let them know what's in store.

You are awake the moment you accept the fact that you are—as each of us is—alone, no matter how many relationships you may have or people you may know.

You are, indeed, special, with capacities that are the pillars of everything worthwhile you will do with your life.

From the moment you are born, the core of your being never changes. Yet how you express yourself can change endlessly, in order to meet life's many demands.

You are moved to give something of value to this world. Not because you were told to, but because you want to. Let it be modest or great; it doesn't matter. Find a way to make a contribution you will be proud of.

You are in the best position to give, and to receive, when you align yourself with people who are your kindred spirits. They will be grateful to you for being who you are, because your life helps them accomplish more with their own. In turn, they will enrich your life by validating those things that are most important to you.

Stand up and be counted. It is the only way people will be able to see you in the fullness of your being. Let the world know what you stand for, and you will become a magnet for like minds and like hearts.

Do these things and you will be rewarded in kind. You will know that you have lived an authentic life, and that you have earned what you have, whether it is money, recognition, love, peace of mind, or, simply, greater self-esteem. Your life will be your legacy. Its totality will be a beacon for your children and for others you have touched along the way.

> *Consider your identity the sun within you, whose energy need never die.*

If people lived by the Identity Credo, relationships would change in dramatic ways. This is particularly true when it comes to families, friends, and work.

Within families, the pressure to be "like" one's father or mother would subside. "You are your own man, your own woman, your own person" would become a mantra of family pride. The idea of being just "one big, happy family" would yield to the notion of being a loving, close-knit clan, whose members honor their differences along with their roots, and need one another as a result of both.

If you consciously chose your friends on the strength of identity, you would forge deeper, longer-lasting bonds. You would actively seek out people who love what you love, and more easily avoid those who have more of what we are all supposed to want: money, status, success. You would forgo popularity for passion, aligning yourself with individuals whose eyes speak with the same clear conviction as your own about the sanctity of identity. Your relationships universe would revolve around the strength of your inner identity circle, not the other way around.

If employers and employees sought to understand, and then act, in a manner that respected one another's identities, we would embrace our jobs more eagerly. The frustration managers express about underperforming people, and the disillusionment people express about out-of-touch managers, would give way to a more urgent, more meaningful dialogue between them.

That dialogue wouldn't be about why people need to "deliver better results," or how management needs to "get its act together." It would be about how the organization can thrive if, and only if, it is populated with individuals who are encouraged to bring their identities to work and to invest them in their organization. In turn, managers would honor and reward people accordingly: not only with money but with heartfelt recognition and an abiding interest in the human being who lives just beneath the skin of the "employee."

In short, there is no person walking this planet who doesn't have the capacity to live through his or her identity. If we were to make identity the foundation of our lives, it would be a better, more productive world. But my vision is at best a hope.

You are the one who matters. You are where the world begins. As you open yourself up to the possibilities your identity code reveals, remember that you are inviolable. You have value in this world simply as a result of being who you are. No one can take your identity away from you. No one can make you be someone you are not. That is your strength and it is eternal.

Never lose sight of who you are.

EPILOGUE:
THE IDENTITY CIRCLE

As you have seen, each part of this book is introduced with a small circle. This circle, which is illustrated fully on page 2, brings together all aspects of the identity code into one integrated figure. This circle, like many, has a long and rich history.

Circles have been invoked for centuries, and by many civilizations, to depict wholeness, eternity, and renewal. In art, the circle, sometimes called a *mandala,* is used in many religious traditions. Some Christian nuns in the twelfth century created many beautiful mandalas to express their beliefs. In the Americas, Native Americans created medicine wheels, while the circular Aztec calendar was both a time-keeping device and a religious expression of ancient Aztecs.

On our planet, living things are made of cells, and each cell has a nucleus. All are circles with centers. Consider a circle with a center the basic structure of creation. It is mirrored in the world, from atoms to the tiniest flowers and spider webs to giant structures, such as our solar system and, within it, the earth.

The circle is more than an image to be seen with our eyes. It is viewed by some cultures to be an actual moment in time—dynamic and fluid, with meaning and purpose. It can be used as a vehicle for exploring not just art and science but life itself.

The Laws of Identity form their own circle, which comes alive with possibilities. You can enter the circle at any point, diving in and coming out, only to reenter it at another place, or another time. At first, the middle of the identity circle appears empty, as though it has no unifying center. Nothing could be further from the truth. You are in the middle. You give the identity circle its meaning. Look deep enough and you will find yourself at its core.

ACKNOWLEDGMENTS

To everyone who contributed to the creation of *The Identity Code,* thank you for inspired thoughts, for believing in the wisdom of identity, and, in many cases, for personifying the power that identity-based living contains. If there are any heroes in my book, they are the people whose stories I relate throughout the text—thank you for being who you are and for being part of my life.

Special acknowledgment goes to a number of individuals whose heartfelt interest in my work—and, sometimes, just an unbiased eye—moved me forward when I needed encouragement.

Thanks to Jim Levine, my agent, who saw the potential in my proposal, understood my drive to popularize the concept of identity, and stayed the course, over nearly two years, to ensure that this book found a home with the right publisher; to Caroline Sutton, my editor, whose eyes, as much as her words, first told me how much she believed in the power of identity, and who has helped bring out the vitality this book contains; to Gerry Sindell, my dear friend and adviser, whose fiery passion for identity matches my own and whose insight and wisdom kept me going when I needed a voice I could trust without reservation.

Finally, I want to offer special thanks to Esra Sertoglu, Thomas

Ordahl, Jim Lowell, and Peter Swerdloff, colleagues from Siegel & Gale. Their personal interest in identity as a framework for living, and their many diverse contributions to this book, have come to mean a great deal to me over the course of the years we've worked together.

ANNOTATED BIBLIOGRAPHY

The literature dedicated to the subject of human identity is vast. There are many books that take aim at identity from different angles, directly and indirectly, spiritually and practically. Here is a list of books I believe offer interesting and useful perspectives on the topic, complementing *The Identity Code.*

Identity Is Destiny, Laurence D. Ackerman (Berrett-Koehler, 2000)

> This is my first book. In it I present the Laws of Identity for the first time and, through the use of case studies and personal narrative, show how people and organizations are governed equally by them.

What Should I Do with My Life?, Po Bronson (Random House, 2002)

> *What Should I Do with My Life?* is written for anyone contemplating major life changes. It is built around dozens of stories about everyday people who have confronted this central question head-on and who have "survived" the challenges that seeking answers bring.

Identity and the Life Cycle, Erik Erikson, (W. W. Norton, 1980)

> In this groundbreaking book, Erikson describes identity as the blending of two forces: an individual's ties with the particular values of his or her family and heritage, and the traits that simply make each

of us special. From his studies, Erikson maps how people grow by developing their identities, beginning in infancy and early child-hood, all the way through to adulthood and mature age.

Wisdom of the Millennium, Helen Exley (Exley Publications, 1999)

This book addresses identity through the lens of many beautiful quotations. It contains some of the wisest words ever written about human values, such as *kindness, hope, courage,* and *perseverance*—the forces of life your identity yields.

The Prophet, Kahlil Gibran (Knopf, 1923)

The Prophet tells the story of a mysterious man who, at the moment of his departure on a journey, wishes to offer people in his village gifts, but he possesses nothing. The people gather round, and each asks a question of the heart. The man's wisdom becomes his gift. The prophet's wisdom touches many of the themes that flow from an identity-based life.

The Soul's Code, James Hillman (Warner Books, 1996)

In this book, Hillman presents a vision of our selves that isn't defined by family relationships or other influences outside of us. He argues that what he terms "character" is fate and goes on to show how the soul, if given the opportunity, can assert itself at an early age. Hillman presents the view that the essence of our indi-viduality is within us from birth, shaping what we do as much as it is shaped by what we do.

Working Identity, Herminia Ibarra (Harvard Business School Press, 2003)

Ibarra's book challenges the traditional belief that a meticulous assessment of one's skills and interests will automatically lead one to discover the right job. Defining the arc of the future is a "never-ending process of putting ourselves through a set of steps that creates and reveals our possible selves." Professor Ibarra shares the stories of twenty-three people who navigated successful career changes.

Self Matters, Phillip C. McGraw, Ph.D. (Simon & Schuster, 2001)

Self Matters challenges people to find their "authentic self"—the person you once were before life took its toll. The book describes this self as a person at his or her greatest, most fulfilled, most real moment—the person one has always wanted to be, but was too distracted, busy, or scared to become.

The Road Less Traveled, M. Scott Peck (Simon & Schuster, 1997)

The author's crucial premise—that life is hard—is challenging for everyone. But through four principles of discipline, Peck argues, we can come to accept and transcend this fact. The "road" the author describes is by no means the easiest, but it is the only one worth taking.

The Book, Alan Watts (Vintage Books, 1966)

The Book delves into what the author perceives as the cause and cure of the illusion that the self is a separate ego, housed in a "bag of skin, which confronts a universe of physical objects that are alien and stupid." This work addresses the nature of the self in ways that are both profound and amusing.

ABOUT THE AUTHOR

LARRY ACKERMAN is a leading authority on organizational and personal identity. He is a group director for Siegel & Gale, an international brand-consulting firm, and widely regarded as the pioneer in the field of identity-based management. In a career spanning nearly twenty-five years, Ackerman has worked to solve some of the most pressing identity challenges facing large organizations, their leaders, and the people they lead. His vision has helped many senior executives discover the right path for their organizations as well as for themselves. As a coach to senior executives as well as a consultant to their organizations, he has used his insights to help many leaders discover the keys not just to survive, but to flourish.

His diverse clients include Alcoa, Maytag, Fidelity Investments, the Dow Chemical Company, Ernst & Young, Boise Cascade, the European beverages giant Interbrew, and the Norwegian industrial concern Norsk Hydro. According to his clients, what gives Mr. Ackerman's work exceptional force is his ability to understand the crucial connections between human identity and organizational identity and to apply this knowledge to help people and companies alike grow and prosper. In his first book, *Identity Is Destiny: Leadership and the Roots of Value Creation,* he set forth a revolutionary view of the nature of identity and its fundamental impact on organizational and personal development.

Mr. Ackerman's articles have appeared in *Journal of Business Strategy, Leaders, Across the Board, Focus on Change Management, US Business Review,* and the American Management Association's *Management Review.* He has been a guest speaker at the Yale School of Management, UCLA Anderson School, and the Wharton School, where he has conducted personal identity development sessions for graduate students. Larry also leads workshops on personal identity for the Learning Annex in New York City. Additionally, he is a regular keynote speaker for senior management meetings among leading global companies. Mr. Ackerman resides in Weston, Connecticut, with his wife, Janet, and his sixteen-year-old son, Max. Contact the author at www.theidentitycode.com.

ABOUT THE TYPE

This book was set in Bembo, a typeface based on an old-style Roman face that was used for Cardinal Bembo's tract *De Aetna* in 1495. Bembo was cut by Francisco Griffo in the early sixteenth century. The Lanston Monotype Machine Company of Philadelphia brought the well-proportioned letter forms of Bembo to the United States in the 1930s.